ENGAGING AND EMPOWERING
Families in Secondary Transition

A Practitioner's Guide

DONNA L. WANDRY AND AMY M. PLEET, EDITORS

Council for
Exceptional
Children

© 2009 by Council for Exceptional Children
All rights reserved.

No part of this publication may be reproduced, stored in a retrieval system, or trans-
mitted, in any form or by any means, electronic, mechanical, photocopying, recording,
or otherwise, without prior written permission of the copyright owner.

Council for Exceptional Children
2900 Crystal Drive, Suite 1000
Arlington, VA 22202
www.cec.sped.org

Library of Congress Cataloging-in-Publication Data

Wandry, Donna L.
Engaging and empowering families in secondary transition. A practitioner's guide / by
Donna L. Wandry and Amy M. Pleet.
p. cm.
Includes biographical references.

ISBN 978-0-86586-445-0 (soft cover edition)
ISBN 978-0-86586-512-9 (eBook edition)

Cover design by Carol Williams.

Layout by Del Moran.

Printed in the United States of America by AGS

First edition

10 9 8 7 6 5 4 3

Contents

CHAPTER 1   **Introduction to the Role of Families in Secondary Transition, 1**
Amy M. Pleet and Donna L. Wandry

Key Definitions, 2
Context of This Publication, 2
The Outcomes Accountability Movement, 3
Foundations of Parent/Family Involvement, 6
The Changing Role of Parents as Partners, 10
A Brief History of Transition Planning and the Parents' Role, 12
Conceptual Framework, 16
Charge to the Reader, 17

CHAPTER 2   **Changing Demographics, 21**
Vicki A. McGinley

Family Structures, 22
Challenges Facing Diverse Families During Transition, 25
Cultural Reciprocity as a Framework, 27
Conclusion, 30

CHAPTER 3   **Parents as Collaborators: Building Partnerships With School- and Community-Based Providers, 33**
Sharon deFur

Developing School-Based, Community-Based, and Family
    Partnerships, 34
What Is a Partnership?, 34
Conclusion, 50

CHAPTER 4   **Parents as Instructors in Their Youths' Emergent Independence, 53**
Michael J. Ward

Benefits of Parents as Instructors, 54
Supporting Parents in the Transfer of Ownership and Advocacy
    to the Adolescent, 54
Challenges in Supporting Parents, 56
Strategies for Fostering Self-Determination in Daily Living
    Activities, 57
Applying the Self-Determination Instructional Partnership
    to Various Domains, 61
Self-Advocacy/Self-Disclosure in Higher Education Settings, 69
Skills Parents Need to Develop, and How Practitioners
    Can Help, 72

CHAPTER 5   **Parents as Evaluators and Decision Makers, 81**
Cherie Takemoto and Cathy Healy

Parents as Evaluators and Decision Makers in Their Child's
    Education Program, 82
Parents as Evaluators and Decision Makers at the System
    Level, 90
Conclusion, 95

CHAPTER 6   **Parents as Peer Mentors, 101**
Suzanne Ripley

Defining "Peer Mentors", 102
Benefits of Parents as Peer Mentors, 102
Considerations in Supporting Parents in Peer Mentor Roles, 104
Mentor Networks and Models, 106
Methods to Engage Parents as Peer Mentors, 110
Conclusion, 116

CHAPTER 7   **Parents as Systems Change Agents, 119**
Mary E. Morningstar

Legal Requirements for Parent Participation, 120
What Is a Systems Change Agent?, 120
Systems Change for Families From Culturally and Linguistically
    Diverse Backgrounds, 122
Systems Change Agents During Transition, 122
Challenges Parents Face as Systems Change Agents, 124
Strategies Supporting Systems Change Agents During
    Transition, 126
Conclusion, 135

CHAPTER 8   **Strategic Engagement for Parent Partnerships, 141**
                Donna L. Wandry and Amy M. Pleet
                Use of Evaluative Tools in This Book, 142
                Making Parent Partnerships a Priority, 142
                Tools for Strategically Building Parent Partnerships, 148
                Final Words, 149

APPENDIX A   **Parent Transition Information Needs Survey, 151**

APPENDIX B   **Degree of Involvement Scale, 152**

APPENDIX C   **Parent Engagement Strategic Planning Guide, 153**

1

Introduction to the Role of Families in Secondary Transition

Amy M. Pleet and Donna L. Wandry

ESSENTIAL QUESTIONS

○ What are the primary legal and historical foundations for providing transition services in schools and for adults?

○ How has the role of families within the transition process evolved?

○ What tools can schools use to evaluate and strategically plan strong parent engagement practices?

Change is constant in education and in adult service provision. As any seasoned educator or service provider will tell you, fads and gimmicks come and go, many without any substantial research base. Those who have been in the trenches for a number of years may say that if you give lip service to the latest trend, it too will pass. This publication is devoted to a "new" movement that has been a long time coming and is not likely to pass, a topic that bears serious consideration by educators and service providers: building partnerships with parents of their students or clients. Research indicates that the ultimate success of these practitioners depends on their ability to build partnerships with parents of youth with disabilities in ways that their training may not have prepared them (Epstein, 2005). There are substantial research data that link thoughtfully implemented parent partnerships with gains in student achievement and other indicators of success (Epstein, 1995, 2005; Epstein, Sanders, & Sheldon; 2007, U.S. Department of Education, 2003). The purpose of this book is to provide to practitioners, working with young adults with disabilities, information and practical strategies that will support them as they build expanded partnerships with parents during the transition years. Further, this second edition provides

1

frameworks for planning and evaluating school- or agency-based practices to build these partnerships.

Key Definitions

First, let us define the terms *parent* and *family*. In this publication, *parent* is intended in a broader sense than biological parents. We use the National PTA's definition of parents: "the adults who play an important role in a child's family life, since other adults—grandparents, aunts, uncles, step-parents, guardians—may carry the primary responsibility for a child's education, development, and well-being" (National PTA, 1997, p. 5). Similarly, the Individuals With Disabilities Education Improvement Act of 2004 (IDEA) defines a parent as

(A) a natural, adoptive, or foster parent of a child (unless a foster parent is prohibited by State law from serving as a parent);

(B) a guardian (but not the State if the child is a ward of the State);

(C) an individual acting in the place of a natural or adoptive parent (including a grandparent, stepparent, or other relative) with whom the child lives, or an individual who is legally responsible for the child's welfare; or

(D) an individual assigned to be a surrogate parent. (20 U.S.C. §1401(23))

Although *Merriam-Webster Online* defines *family* as "the basic unit in society traditionally consisting of two parents rearing their children; . . . *also:* any of various social units differing from but regarded as equivalent to the traditional family" (2009a), our usage is aligned with the previous broader definitions of parents.

Merriam-Webster Online defines *partnership* as "a relationship resembling a legal partnership and usually involving close cooperation between parties having specified and joint rights and responsibilities" (2009b). Within a practitioner–family partnership, there are a number of joint responsibilities as all parties cooperate in supporting the young adult with disabilities to make a successful transition into adult life. There are also specified responsibilities—some assumed by the school or adult service agency and others assumed by the family. The specifics of the partnership will vary with the individual's disability, goals, and family circumstances.

Context of This Publication

We are living in the midst of a paradigm shift in the service industries regarding accountability. Educators and adult service providers historically have provided services to students or clients with their accountability measures based on whether or not the services were provided. For example, they reported simply how many students received special education services and where, or the number of young adults who completed a vocational assessment. In the new paradigm, evaluative measures focus on the results produced by these services, that is, the outcomes or "results." This focus is at the core of recent legislation like IDEA and the No Child Left

Behind Act of 2001 (NCLB), which require school systems and states to report student outcome data to the federal government and make their outcomes visible to parents. As a result, schools must now report disaggregated state test scores of students receiving special education services and the number of evaluated youth who entered a career training program, as well as "customer satisfaction" with the services. This shift into an outcome context, as a result of legislative actions, has produced myriad changes in practices within the educational and adult service systems.

The Outcomes Accountability Movement

Government Performance and Results Act of 1993

In 1993, President Clinton signed into law the Government Performance and Results Act (GPRA). This act required all organizations that received federal funding to establish performance measures and then track and report their results. Each agency was required to (a) set program goals; (b) measure performance against those goals; (c) report progress publicly; (d) improve program effectiveness and accountability by promoting a new focus on results, service quality, and customer satisfaction; and (e) improve service delivery by planning to meet program objectives and providing information about program results and service quality.

The passage of GPRA was not a surprise. For some time, political and lobbying groups had publicized misuse of public funds and called for accountability measures. Nonetheless, organizations and agencies were caught off guard. They found themselves debating what their outcomes ultimately were and grappling with how to measure them. For airports, the discussion centered on not how many planes took off, but on how many took off on time, how many accidents occurred, and how many pieces of luggage were lost and ultimately found. For the post office, the discussion shifted from how many pieces of mail were processed to how many pieces were misdirected and how long customers had to stand in line for service. The context shifted from routine operations to a focus on customer satisfaction and met needs.

The U.S. Department of Education (ED) shifted from a focus on whether the teachers delivered the curriculum to whether the students were gaining in knowledge and skills. ED (2001) announced four goals to meet the GPRA requirements:

1. Help all students reach challenging academic standards so that they are prepared for responsible citizenship, further learning, and productive employment.
2. Build a solid foundation for learning for all children.
3. Ensure access to post-secondary education and lifelong learning.
4. Make the United State Department of Education a high performance organization by focusing on results, service quality, and customer satisfaction.

These four goals established a model for states and local school systems to focus on outcomes that would be needed to achieve the challenge of

GPRA. Today, the U.S. Office of Management and Budget uses Program Assessment Rating Tools (PART, 2007) for every program receiving federal funding to

> assess and improve a program's effectiveness and efficiency. The quality check process will review PART programs to ensure they have consistent, reasonably aggressive and outcome-oriented performance goals. These goals are used in program assessments and evaluations and are the focus of attention by stakeholders, program managers, departments and agencies, Congress and future Administrations. (Office of Management and Budget, 2008)

No Child Left Behind Act of 2001

George W. Bush, upon taking office, announced the NCLB as the priority of his administration's domestic agenda. Upon its passage in 2001, which amended the Elementary and Secondary Education Act of 1994, it came to be considered as "one of the most sweeping changes to education in a generation" (Murdick, Gartin, & Crabtree, 2007, p. 34). Four overriding national policy goals formed the context for NCLB: equal opportunity, full participation, independent living, and economic self-sufficiency (A. Turnbull, Turnbull, & Wehmeyer, 2007). Using as its charge the desire to improve educational results and hold schools accountable for meeting high academic standards (A. Turnbull et al.; Yell & Drasgow, 2005), the firm assumption of the mandate was that high expectations coupled with meeting academic competencies would produce more active, productive adults (Bassett & Kochhar-Bryant, 2002). The tangible outgrowth of that assumption was the development of accountability measures, in the form of high-stakes testing tied to rigorous state academic standards.

Further direction was given within NCLB through guiding principles: (a) accountability for student growth, indicated through adequate yearly progress (AYP) showing systematic improvement at the school level toward 100% proficiency in academic standards by 2014; (b) accountability for highly qualified teachers, indicated through meeting proficiency standards before being certified; (c) accountability in local flexibility of how funds are to be used to meet NCLB outcome expectations; (d) accountability for safe schools to facilitate learning; and (e) accountability for opportunity provision to parents for educational participation, evaluation, and decision making (R. Turnbull, Huerta, & Stowe, 2006; Yell & Drasgow, 2005). It is these guiding principles that were heeded when IDEA (2004) was crafted, in an effort to reduce NCLB/IDEA conflict (Murdick et al., 2007).

Individuals With Disabilities Education Improvement Act of 2004

The Individuals With Disabilities Education Act of 1997 reflected the outcomes focus of GPRA. State and local special education programs were required to conduct a comprehensive self-evaluation process. With specific criteria to address, each local educational agency (LEA) assembled stakeholder groups to identify outcomes and outcome measures, then proceeded to design and implement a self-evaluation process. No longer would it be sufficient to have students' special education folders ready when the U.S. Office of Special Education Programs (OSEP) representatives came for the scheduled monitoring visits. Of course, the monitors would still be concerned with whether due process measures had been met as documented within the student folders, but now they would also be looking for documentation that student outcomes were improving. Data were gathered related to graduation rate, participation in general education programs, and performance on state- and district-level progress measures. Many states began follow-up or longitudinal studies on postschool outcomes of students with disabilities. Each LEA began the process of gathering input from stakeholder groups with strong parent participation. Special Education Advisory Boards, with 50% parents or individuals with disabilities as members, became influential. Parents shared their stories in interviews, surveys, and testimony, and their broad awareness of the whole life of their child impacted decisions made by special education leaders. The question shifted from "Are we following regulations in providing services?" to "Are we providing required services in ways that provide optimum student benefit?"

IDEA 2004, following the lead of NCLB (2002), further strengthened the focus on outcomes measures. The major purposes of the law were redefined to address barriers perceived to have plagued prior versions: low expectations and insufficient application of research on proven teaching and learning methods for students with disabilities. The accountability constructs established by NCLB set high expectations for all students in the general education curriculum while assessing their proficiency relative to that curriculum and was the conduit for IDEA embracing NCLB as a partner in addressing perceived weaknesses within its own accountability system.

To provide outcome measures for these concerns, as well as other aspects of special education service provision, IDEA 2004 required all states to develop a State Performance Plan (SPP) describing how they would implement the Act's requirements and purposes and improve results for students with disabilities. In addition to the 6-year SPP (covering 2005–2010), IDEA required each state to develop and submit an Annual Performance Report (APR) describing its progress in meeting the targets established in the SPP. As a way to organize these data, states were asked to respond to 20 performance indicators addressing three areas:

(A) Provision of a free appropriate public education in the least restrictive environment.

(B) State exercise of general supervisory authority, including child find, effective monitoring, the use of resolution sessions, mediation, voluntary binding arbitration, and a system of transition services . . . .

(C) Disproportionate representation of racial and ethnic groups in special education and related services, to the extent the representation is the result of inappropriate identification. (20 U.S.C. §1416, Sec. 616(a)(3))

Of particular importance to the goals of this book is Indicator 8, which charges states to give clear accountability measures on parent participation; specifically, it requires data on the percentage of parents with a child receiving special education services who report that schools "facilitated parent involvement as a means of improving services and results for children with disabilities" [20 U.S.C. 1416(a)(3)(A)]. During the last decade, it has become clear that parent involvement in the special education process is not to be undervalued or underdeveloped; conversely, the mandatory language has moved steadily forward in not only placing parents in valuable positions within the process, but also in requiring data showing that parent involvement is indeed happening.

Foundations of Parent/Family Involvement

Epstein's Research on Parent Involvement in Education

For over two decades, Joyce Epstein, Director of the Center on School, Family, and Community Partnerships at Johns Hopkins University, has been leading research on types, outcomes, and methods of promoting parent involvement in education. Her early research into the effectiveness of school programs, the extent of family influence, and the impact of socioeconomic community conditions on the success of students revealed that these three forces could not be clearly distinguished (Epstein, 1996). She proposed that school, communities, and families have overlapping spheres of influence on children. Further, she advocated for partnerships to be formed between the three entities, mutually responsible to create better programs and opportunities for students. These partnerships must view the child holistically, requiring the influence of each sphere in order to "engage, guide, energize, and motivate students to produce their own successes" (Epstein, 1995, p. 702).

In the evolution of the parent involvement movement, Epstein states, "The first frameworks focused mainly on the roles that parents needed to play and not the work that schools needed to conduct in order to organize strong programs to involve all families in their children's education" (Epstein, 1996, p. 211). This description mirrors the evolution of parent involvement in transition planning, placing the burden of responsibility for partnership on parents, rather than on the school. Our analysis of special education mandates and accountability (see Chapter 8) reveals a focus on parent rights and visibility in the process, but not on schools building a reciprocal partnership between schools and families.

In 1996, Epstein reported that the underlying research question in general education had moved from, "Are families important for student success in school," to "*If* families are important for children's development and school success, *how* can schools help all families conduct the activities that will benefit their children?" (p. 213). The research of the National Center on Families, Communities, Schools and Children's Learning, created in 1990 by the federal government at Johns Hopkins University under Epstein's leadership, included over 20 researchers from several disciplines. Using varied methods and measurement models, they worked closely with educators and parents to design and study new approaches for productive partnerships (Epstein, 1996). The Center created an International Network of over 300 researchers in the United States and more than 40 nations "to encourage and to share work on many topics related to school, family, and community partnerships" (Epstein, 1996, p. 212). Through this collaborative venture, studies

> began to clarify the amorphous term *parent involvement,* and recast the emphasis from parent involvement (left up to the parent) . . . *to school, family, and community partnerships* . . . . The concept of "shared responsibility" removed part of the burden from parents to figure out independently how to become or stay involved in their children's education from year to year and put part of that burden on schools to create programs to inform and involve all families. (Epstein, 1996, p. 211; see also Epstein & Salinas, 2004)

The result of this research has led to a shifting context for parent involvement in education.

Schools, districts, and states joining the National Network of Partnership Schools, (NNPS), based at Johns Hopkins University under the leadership of Epstein, submit information about their partnership practices and their student achievement data. In return, they are given training and technical assistance in infusing strategies for strong partnerships within their improvement plans. In 2003, NNPS initiated a 5-year longitudinal study of 400 schools in 50 districts, to assess the effects of the NNPS intervention model on family and community involvement to support student achievement in reading, math, and science. The project will "scale up" professional development tools, guidelines, and approaches for curriculum-linked involvement activities that have been developed, pilot tested, and shown to (a) produce systemic and sustained change in district and school knowledge, policies, and programs of school, family, and community partnerships; (b) effectively improve the involvement of parents and the community; and (c) increase student reading, math, and science achievement, and other indicators of student success (Epstein et al., 2007).

In a review of research on the relationship between parent involvement and student reading proficiency, Sheldon and Epstein (2005) concluded that the critical factor was whether schools designed and implemented quality parent involvement activities targeted at giving parents skills to support their child's literacy skills acquisition. Further, they stated,

> Research on a nationally representative sample of secondary students show that, after controlling for prior levels of achievement, students tend to score higher on reading achievement tests and/or earn higher grades in English if their parents have discussions with them about school and about their future plans, check their homework, and maintain high educational expectations. (p. 119)

They reported similar findings relative to math achievement: "Students in neighborhoods with high concentrations of poverty had had lower math achievement test scores, but this effect was ameliorated by on-going parent involvement in high schools" (Epstein & Sheldon, 2006, p. 10).

In their call for additional research on parent partnership practices and results, Epstein and Sheldon (2006) provide evidence that when school improvement plans incorporate goals and specific actions to promote targeted parent engagement, with support and technical assistance from the district, these activities are more likely to be conducted and gains in student achievement are more likely to be found. All these research findings point towards benefits of building a systematic approach to engaging parents within the transition process.

Transition Implications of Epstein's Research

Research findings from the Johns Hopkins National Center make six contributions to improving transition outcomes for students with disabilities. First, the research has shown that partnerships contribute to increased student achievement. Second, the research confirms that parent involvement tends to decline across the grades, unless schools and teachers work to develop and implement appropriate practices of partnerships at each grade. Third, the research indicates that teachers' practices to involve families are as or more important than family background variables such as race or ethnicity, social class, marital status, or mother's work status for determining whether and how parents become involved in their children's education. That is, schools and teachers who practice strategies for building parent partnerships can have more influence on the involvement of parents than family background variables. Fourth, the research has documented that there are subject-specific links between the involvement of families and increases in achievement by students. For example, studies of teacher practices to involve parents with in-home reading activities report more involvement in family reading and improved student reading scores. Fifth, not all activities to involve families lead quickly or directly to increased student outcomes. Instead, for example, interactions about parenting skills during transition years would first be expected to affect parents' informal interactions with their young adults. If families continue to influence or reinforce students' attitudes, behaviors, or motivation, then student outcomes may increase over time. And sixth, the research has shown that all parties want more partnerships between schools, families, and communities, but most don't know how (Epstein, 1995, 1996; Pleet, 2000).

Epstein's Six Types of Parent Involvement (Epstein, 1995; Epstein & Salinas, 2004) emerged from this extensive research, and provide a useful framework for developing partnerships with families. Each type has applications for transition planning (Pleet, 2000).

1. *Parenting activities* equip parents with the information, skills, and supports to be effective parents to their adolescents with disabilities during the transition years. These activities address questions such as: What do I need to know as a parent about the adult service eligibility system so that I can assure that my teenager will be able to access needed supports and services? How do we provide guidance to our teenagers as they make choices about future employment, further education, and independent living? How do we coach our teenagers as they develop self-determination skills so needed for their future?

2. *Communication activities* must be two-way, regular, and meaningful. Schools and adult providers should inform parents about upcoming events and proposed program or system reforms. In order to be two-

way, these activities provide opportunities for input from parents and interagency organizations. The public forums required under IDEA 2004 and the Rehabilitation Act Amendments of 1998 are examples of communication activities. Most important, schools establish reciprocal channels of communication about each individual student's issues, goals, and progress.

3. *Volunteering activities* include opportunities for parents to support school goals and student learning "in any way, at any place, and at any time—not just during the school day and at the school building" (Epstein, 1996, p. 705). Parents might contact their own employers to arrange for job shadowing or field trip opportunities for students, organize parent support networks, or serve on an advisory boards. The role of the school is to (a) recruit volunteers from all parents, (b) provide for schedule flexibility, (c) address training needs, (d) match parent talents with school and student needs, and (e) recognize the efforts of parents. The view of volunteering presented here is quite different from the old paradigm of parents volunteering at a bake sale.

4. *Learning at home activities* are designed to engage parents as partners in the learning the students do outside of the school or adult training facility. One activity that has yielded positive results for students and for schools is to expand "homework" to include interactive assignments students are to complete with family members. For example, a homework assignment might be to interview two working adults in your home or community about the process that led to their career choices. Schools also provide guidance to parents as to the expectations for their role in homework, "encouraging, listening, reacting, praising, guiding, monitoring, and discussing—not teaching" (Epstein, 1995, p. 705).

5. *Decision-making activities* include parents in school decisions and develop parent leaders and representatives. IDEA 2004 requires special education advisory panels comprising more than 50% parents or individuals with disabilities. These panels provide decision-making opportunities for parents, but the challenge for schools will be to promote similar opportunities for all parents of students receiving special education services. Schools need to create multiple strategies to engage parents in the development and evaluation of special education programs and services, listening to a wide range of parents—not just those who would rubber-stamp administrative proposals.

6. *Collaborating with community activities* have significant importance for families during the transition years. Transition planning for each student who receives special education services, beginning no later than the age of 16 (14 in some states) requires consideration of work-based learning opportunities, community-based learning opportunities, and linkages with community and adult services. The challenge in this type of parent involvement is to develop strategies that empower the student and integrate resources—and yet keep the parent involved. One example of Type 6 is producing a transition fair with adult and college support services and employers. Another example is an organized field trip for parents and students to the local community college for an orientation to services, course expectations, and financial aid.

Using this framework does not mean coordinating six different activities; one strategically planned activity may incorporate several types of parent involvement. For example, if a school or adult agency sponsors a parent-organized, parent-to-parent mentoring program, this activity could have dimensions that fit at least Types 1, 2, and 3. Epstein's research is the basis for the National Standards for Family-School Partnerships (National PTA, 2007), as well as a primary foundation for the conceptual framework for this book.

The Changing Role of Parents as Partners

Parent Role Changes Across Education

As a result of the research of Epstein and others, a conceptual shift is occurring across education related to parent involvement. Parents had historically been viewed as a cadre of volunteers for the school, primarily responsible for ensuring that their children came to school ready to learn. With the publication of Goals 2000 (Educate America Act of 1994) came the charge of Goal 8: "By the year 2000 . . . every school will promote partnerships that will increase parental involvement and participation in promoting the social, emotional, and academic growth of children" (20 U.S.C. § 580, Sec. 102(8)(A)). NCLB, further expanding the role of parents,

> requires districts and schools to involve families in ways that will boost student achievement. Yet, most districts and schools are struggling with how to implement effective partnership programs and how to measure the "value added" effects of family and community involvement for student achievement in specific subjects. (Epstein et al., 2007)

In the best situations, as school leaders developed plans to build these partnerships, they realized that in any partnership, the partners come with complementary but different levels of expertise, skills, and knowledge. Yet, they come together with common vision and goals. They recognized that partnerships must be built on open communication, trust, and flexibility, and must focus on collaborative problem solving and strategy design. Within this new view of the role of parents, educational leaders began to design new approaches to offer parents opportunities. Schools welcomed parents into efforts to meet the national goals to assist students to achieve challenging academic standards in preparation for responsible citizenship, lifelong learning, and productive employment (GPRA, 1993). Many school leaders acknowledged that partnership with parents was critical.

Unfortunately, there were also school leaders who resisted building partnerships with parents. Their role as the expert in educational matters was threatened as they were confronted with the new paradigm. These educators enjoyed the superiority and security of having the answers at the back of the book, of being the teachers who delivered subject matter to "eager and willing" open learners. They might lose control of their classrooms if they organized learning in response to different learning styles with interactive or differentiated learning strategies. They were afraid of what would happen if they "lowered" themselves to include parents on school reform committees as equal partners. They held parents at arms' length, giving them only the most basic of information without revealing the deep-seated issues underlying school reform dilemmas.

Parents either backed off and became silent, acquiescing members, or became aggressive in their determination to be heard (Garriott, Wandry, & Snyder, 2000). Many parents spoke at school board meetings, wrote letters to newspapers, and refused to accept inadequate education for their children. Some educational leaders took deliberate measures to reduce the impact of these parents. Administrators discouraged teachers from "leaking" information to parents ("no need to air our dirty linens in public"). One principal refused to allow a teacher to conduct a parent information night because "an armed parent is a dangerous parent" (anonymous, personal communication, c. 2000). Davies (2002) conducted research to compare practices he had observed in 1996 with current practices of involving parents as partners in education. He noted a change in the presence of the language of partnership; politicians, educational leaders, advocates, and conferences all highlighted family involvement and partnership. On the other hand, he said, "practices in most schools have hardly caught up with the flourishing rhetoric" (p. 389). The first of his seven recommendations is that teachers and principals must join together in designing the partnership approaches to be used.

Parent Role Changes in Special Education

While the paradigm shift in parent involvement was occurring in general education, a parallel shift was happening in special education. Beginning with the Education for All Handicapped Children Act of 1975, schools were required to involve parents in the identification, assessment, and individualized program decisions for their children with disabilities. The process could not occur without parental consent—but this was not the same thing as building partnerships with parents. GPRA (1993), Goals 2000 (1994), and, later, NCLB (2002) influenced legislators developing the reauthorization of IDEA 1997 and 2004. The regulations and monitoring requirements of IDEA 2004 clearly directed state and LEAs to build partnerships with parents.

The enhanced requirements for building partnerships with parents in the regulations of IDEA 2004 can be grouped into six categories:

1. States must ensure that the rights of parents are protected and complaint procedures and safeguard procedures for the child's individualized education program (IEP) are disseminated and implemented. There are enhanced documentation requirements for school attempts to secure parental participation in IEP planning meetings.

2. The majority of members of any State Advisory Panel (appointed by the governor in most states) must be individuals with disabilities or parents of children with disabilities. This Panel advises the state educational agency on the unmet needs of students with disabilities. It comments publicly on the rules or regulations proposed by the state and advises the state on developing evaluative measures and reporting data to OSEP. The Panel also advises the state on developing corrective action plans to address findings identified in federal monitoring reports and advises the state educational agency on developing and imple-

menting policies related to coordinating services for students with disabilities. Finally, the State Advisory Panel conducts meetings available to the public and submits an annual report to the state. LEAs are required to have local advisory boards as well (20 U.S.C. §1412, Sec. 612(21)(B)).

3. Parents are integral to the State and Local Performance Plans. In both plans, IDEA mandates that there must be provision for joint training of parents, special educators, related service providers, and general education personnel.

4. Parent counseling and training is a related service available as needed within the IEP. This service is defined as "assisting parents in understanding the special needs of their child, providing parents with information about child development, and helping parents to acquire the necessary skills to allow them to support the implementation of their child's IEP" (20 U.S.C. §1412, Sec. 300.34(c)(B)(iii)).

5. Monitoring of local school systems and nonpublic placements is a complex process with many component parts. One of the required parts is direct information from parents. This may include parent questionnaires or other methods to gain parent perspectives on the effectiveness of special education services and programs. Special education leaders must show how parent input was obtained and used in evaluation and improvement plans.

6. IDEA provides funding for parent training and information centers and community resource centers in each state to provide technical assistance, information, and referrals so that parents can "develop the skills necessary to cooperatively and effectively participate in educational planning and decision making" (20 U.S.C. §1470. Sec. 670(1)(2)(3)).

A Brief History of Transition Planning and the Parents' Role

Evolution of Transition Planning Requirements in IDEA

In her 1984 policy paper, "Bridges from School to Working Life," Madeleine Will, Assistant Secretary of the U.S. Department of Education Office of Special Education and Rehabilitation Services (OSERS), and herself a parent of a child with a disability, spoke of services needed to help students with disabilities make the transition from secondary education to adult life. She encouraged schools and adult service agencies to address the complex issues that students and families face as they navigate this transition. Professional conferences and publications delineated the issues, proposed strategies, and described programs designed to assist students and their families—but these transition discussions were generally held separately. IDEA 1990 required schools to include transition planning as a component in IEP planning. The guidelines for establishing transition goals on the IEP by age 16, tying them to other goals and objectives, or implementing interagency partnerships were not particularly well defined, nor were measures to ensure any degree of quality.

The reauthorization of IDEA in 1997 shifted the focus for transition planning. The purpose of the special education law added an additional phrase (in italics): The purpose of special education was to "provide a free appropriate public education (FAPE) designed to meet their unique needs and *prepare them for further education, employment and independent living*" (20 U.S.C. §1400(c)(5)(A)(i)). With this shift in focus, partly in response to GPRA (1993), transition was not considered an add-on conversation, but rather the initial conversation in the IEP planning process. In other words, once the student reached 14 (or earlier, if appropriate) the IEP team would (a) establish the student's interests and future goals as a context for the student's individualized planning process, (b) examine the student's present levels of performance, transition service needs (in a course of study), and needed transition services (in a coordinated set of activities), and (c) develop annual goals and objectives (Storms, O'Leary, & Williams, 2000). IEP teams began to realize how crucial parent input was to this new process. Parents had important contributions to make to discussions about their own children's hopes, dreams, present performance, and goals. Parents and guardians generally become the case managers for the young adult with disabilities as they move to services beyond high school. In addition to the case management role, parents assist in helping their children to clarify postschool goals and articulate needs and preferences (Wehmeyer, Palmer, Agran, Mithaug, & Martin, 2000). Further, the language was clear regarding age of majority rights for students with disabilities to be shared during transition planning; this helped prepare parents in advance to preclude unnecessary guardianship applications or misunderstanding of the parental role in the transition planning process (Lindsey, Wehmeyer, Guy, & Martin, 2001; Test, Aspel, & Everson, 2006).

IDEA 2004 brought a change in timelines and a slight shift in focus relative to transition planning. Rather than requiring the onset of transition planning at age 14, the 2004 requirement shifted the onset of formal planning to no later than the first IEP in place at age 16. The Act offered a clarification of FAPE as a path to preparation for further education (newly added), employment, and independent living. In addition, it shifted transition language from an outcomes-oriented process to a results-oriented process, grounded in measurable IEP goals stemming from age-appropriate assessments. These alterations reinforced the new marriage between IDEA and NCLB, both in terms of expected outcomes and performance measurement. Despite concerns, though, about the perceived dichotomy between heavy accountability to performance and the tenets of transition programming vis-a-vis course of study and instructional activities, the pervasive mindset being supported is that these are not dichotomous ideas, but rather may be viewed as symbiotic pathways to postschool success (Bassett & Kochhar-Bryant, 2002; Patton & Trainor, 2002; Wehmeyer, Sands, Knowlton, & Kozleski, 2002).

Although the vision of transition as a student/family-centered process continued under the mandates of IDEA 2004, practitioners were not always accurate in perceptions of families relative to the transition process. Wandry and colleagues (2008) surveyed preservice teachers on their perceptions of barriers and facilitators to effective transition practices they had encountered in field and teaching experiences. One relevant finding indicated that family involvement was regarded as the most crucial conduit to effective transition planning, and correspondingly that the lack of such involvement was a prime barrier to effective transition programming. The caution of this finding is that practitioners may blame parents for ineffective transition planning and implementation rather than recognize their own responsibility for engaging parents in the process.

NLTS2 Findings Related to Parent Involvement

The National Longitudinal Transition Study 2 (Newman, 2005) examined school factors and postschool outcomes of youth with disabilities. NLTS2 investigated a nationally representative sample of more than 11,000 youth who on December 1, 2000, were ages 13 through 16, receiving special education, and in at least seventh grade. Information was gathered from parents/guardians of NLTS2 youth in telephone interviews or through mail questionnaires in the spring and summer of 2001, 2003, and 2005. Combined, these responses provide a national picture of the extent of parent participation in the education of their children with disabilities (see Table 1 for responses to selected questions).

Parents of the sample population were surveyed in three waves (2001, 2003, and 2005) to gather their perspectives on their involvement in various capacities during their children's transition years. Although there was a trend as the sample population grew older for parents to report increasing satisfaction with the amount they were involved in the IEP process, there was also a trend for these parents to less frequently attend those IEP meetings or other meetings of support groups and parent information training centers. Parents also reported little increase in student participation or leadership in the IEP meeting. Although other findings of the NLTS2 provide valuable data to make conclusions about in school and community variables that influence successful postschool outcomes, we believe that these data are inconclusive and provide a tenuous platform at best for establishing viable parent partnerships.

Rehabilitation Act/Workforce Investment Act Requirements

In 1998 the reauthorization of the Rehabilitation Act of 1973 also incorporated requirements for reporting outcomes and for building partnerships with parents of clients. The passage of the Rehabilitation Act Amendments of 1998 as a component of the larger Workforce Investment Partnership Act of 1998 (WIPA) largely reinforced the earlier 1993 reauthorization regulations encouraging client and family involvement. In addition, several changes in the 1998 amendments reinforced the partnership message.

Within the WIPA itself (now referred to as Workforce Investment Act, WIA; 20 U.S.C. §9201), the key action of establishing youth councils within local Workforce Investment Boards (Section 117, Title I) demonstrated a strong commitment to consumer input. WIA also required the Rehabilitation Services Administration (RSA) to become a partner in the one-stop service delivery system mandated by WIPA (Section 121). This practice, grounded in interagency information sharing, was designed to simplify employment-related adult service agency access by consumers—which in turn was intended to have a positive effect on the ability of agencies and

TABLE 1: Findings of the National Longitudinal Transition Study 2

Parent Responses	2001	2003	2005
Involvement in the IEP process			
• Were involved about the right amount	64.9%	69.4%	74%
• Would like to be more involved	33.7%	29.3%	24.9%
Adult met with teachers to set postsecondary goal	49.0%	—	—
Adult went to IEP meeting for special education program in the current or prior year	88.4%	87.1%	85.0%
IEP goals are strong and challenging for youth (agree or strongly agree)	88.2%	88.0%	89.3%
Adult spoke with youth about his/her school experiences (regularly)	81.7%	72.5%	83.7%
Student participation in IEP meeting			
• Youth present/ participated little	34.0%	28.8%	35.4%
• Youth provided some input	50.2%	49.3%	45.7%
• Youth took a leadership role	15.8%	21.9%	18.8%
Adult provided assistance with homework			
• 5 or more times per week[a]	21.3%	12.2%	7.9%
• 3–4 times per week	21.2%	16.6%	13.3%
• 1–2 times per week	33.2%	34.1%	28.3%
• Less than once per week[b]	12.7%	20.0%	21.4%
• Never	11.5%	17.2%	29.2%
Adult volunteered at the school (1 or more times)	23.8%	20.1%	17.4%
Belongs to support groups for families of youth with disabilities	9.4%	8.6%	7.0%
Attended meetings/trainings supported by parent information training center (yes)	41.6%	38.1%	40.3%

Note. IEP = Individualized education program. Dash indicates that data were not obtained or reported.
[a]Parents of youth without disabilities = 4%. [b]Parents of youth without disabilities = 45%.

consumers to work together in expediting the application and eligibility determination process.

The Rehabilitation Act of 1993 and the Amendments of 1998 had several components to potentially strengthen the partnerships between agency providers and consumers and their families. Specifically, a youth in transition (who was an applicant or eligible client of the RSA) engaged in developing the Individual Plan for Employment (IPE) was provided (a) information on increased options, and (b) technical assistance in developing the IPE as well as other pertinent information. Client empowerment was further evident in the principle of *informed choice*. Although the regulatory language (Section 361.52, now subsumed into the Workforce Investment Act of 1998) purposely did not define this term, the intent was clear in the increased empowerment of those accessing rehabilitation services, and the responsibility of RSA to provide adequate information to support informed choice making.

Systemically, the Rehabilitation Act of 1993 and its 1998 Amendments offered regulatory language that strengthened the voice of the consumers and their families. Within the due process arena, the Act was clear in its intent to provide effective mediation and impartial hearing rights for applicants or eligible individuals and their representatives (Section 361.57) dissatisfied with planned or provided services. Representation within systemic structures also increased, in that State Rehabilitation Councils were required to include a representative of a parent training and information center. This presence was particularly important, because the Council, in consultation with the Workforce Investment Board, was empowered to engage in program evaluation and systemic change.

Finally, the Rehabilitation Act and its Amendments offered direct service to families of applicants and eligible individuals, in recognition of the potential for family involvement in the rehabilitation process. Specifically, vocational rehabilitation services were available, as necessary, to family members to enable the client to achieve an employment outcome. This family partnership also was a basis for providing training and technical assistance in the use of assistive technology, recognizing that family support may be necessary to develop the client's proficiency across settings.

The language and the intent of WIA and the Rehabilitation Act and its Amendments evinced strong roots in consumer and family empowerment. The challenge before us is the translation of language and intent into practices that truly embrace these partnerships.

Conceptual Framework

The conceptual framework for this book is built upon three beliefs:

- Parents need to be fully informed partners in education and adult service provision.
- It is the practitioner's responsibility to empower parents to emerge as partners in ways that are individually appropriate to the family's circumstances.
- It is the parents' responsibility to become accountable for action upon and within the system.

The chapters of this book address family systems, structures, and sociological context (Chapter 2), and the roles that parents can and should play during the transition years, both in school and adult service agencies (Chapters 3–7). These roles are:

1. Parents as collaborators in the IEP process
2. Parents as instructors in their youth's emergent independence
3. Parents as decision makers and evaluators
4. Parents as peer mentors

5. Parents as systems change agents

The chapters develop, within each role, a vision of effective parent activities, success indicators, the challenges faced by parents, and research-based strategies to empower parents.

Charge to the Reader

Although there is little disagreement about the importance of having parents as full partners in the transition process, there has historically been a lack of evidence that schools are proactively building these partnerships. We believe that practitioners need preservice and inservice professional development to gain the knowledge, skills, and dispositions underpinning these partnerships. Additionally, this book can be seen as a tool to critically assess levels of parent involvement in school and agency settings, and to pragmatically plan steps to personally or organizationally facilitate more empowered parent partnerships. Appendix A's Parent Transition Information Needs Survey is a tool to be given to parents prior to IEP meetings that will include discussion of transition issues; Appendix B's Degree of Involvement Scale is a tool that practitioners can use to determine the extent of involvement for individual parents relative to our five roles; and Appendix C's Parent Engagement Strategic Planning Guide is an evaluation tool that practitioners can use to identify proactive strategies that are currently in place or missing. In addition, the authors of each chapter have included specific evidence-based strategies to assist schools, districts, and programs in moving from a willing stance into action, as well as illustrations of promising practices implemented in local districts, schools, or agencies. Practitioners can use each chapter's Indicators of Success as a self-assessment of their own competencies and practices.

We challenge you, our readers, whether you are involved in educational or adult service provision for youth with disabilities. As practitioners in the transition process, you hold the power to empower families to emerge as full partners. Your attitude and your actions will speak louder than your words. When parents reflect on their contact with you, what will they say? Will they say you gave them the knowledge and skills to become collaborators, instructors in their youth's emergent independence, decision makers and evaluators, peer mentors, and system change agents? Will they say you supported their efforts to become more effective parents and influential members of the community? Will they say you made a difference in their family's partnership with professionals? Our intent is that this book will give you useful tools. We know every tool won't produce the same results with every family. We entrust you to use your professional judgment and creativity to design strategies that work and share your successes and lessons learned with your colleagues. Together we can build strong partnerships with parents that will build improved outcomes for young adults with disabilities.

REFERENCES

Bassett, D., & Kochhar-Bryant, C. (2002). Future directions for transition and standards-based education. In C. Kochhar-Bryant & D. Bassett (Eds.), *Aligning transition and standards-based education: Issues and strategies* (pp. 187–202). Arlington, VA: Council for Exceptional Children.

Davies, D. (2002). The 10th school revisited: Are school/family/community partnerships on the reform agenda now? *Phi Delta Kappan, 83,* 388–392.

Education for All Handicapped Children Act of 1975, 20 U.S.C. § 1400 *et seq.* (1975).

Epstein, J. L. (1995). School/family/community partnerships. *Phi Delta Kappan,* 701–712.

Epstein, J. L. (1996). Perspectives and previews on research and policy for school, family, and community partnerships. In A. Booth & J. F. Dunn (Eds.), *Family-school links: How do they affect educational outcomes?* (pp. 209–246). Mahwah, NJ: Erlbaum.

Epstein, J. L. (2005, September). *Developing and sustaining research-based programs of school, family, and community partnerships: Summary of five years of NNPS research.* Retrieved July 9, 2008, from http://www.csos.jhu.edu/P2000/pdf/Research%20Summary.pdf

Epstein, J. L., & Salinas, K. C. (2004). Partnering with families and communities. *Educational Leadership, 26*(8), 12–18.

Epstein, J. L., Sanders, M. G., & Sheldon, S. B. (2007). *Family and community involvement: Achievement effects.* Retrieved July 9, 2008, from http://www.csos.jhu.edu/P2000/pdf/NICHD%20Progress%20Report%20Summary%2007.pdf

Epstein, J. L., & Sheldon, S. B. (2006). Moving forward: Ideas for research on school, family, and community partnerships. In C. F. Conrad & R. Serlin (Eds.), *SAGE Handbook for research in education: Engaging ideas and enriching inquiry* (pp. 117–137). Thousand Oaks, CA: Sage.

Garriott, P., Wandry, D., & Snyder, L. (2000). Teachers as parents, parents as children: What's wrong with this picture? *Preventing School Failure, 45*(1), 37–43.

Goals 2000: Educate America Act of 1994, 20 U.S.C. § 5801 *et seq.* (1994).

Government Performance and Results Act of 1993, 31 U.S.C. § 1101 *et seq.* (1993).

Individuals With Disabilities Education Improvement Act of 2004, 20 U.S.C. §§1400 *et seq.* (2004).

Lindsey, P., Wehmeyer, M. L., Guy, B., & Martin, J. (2001). Age of majority and mental retardation: A position statement of the Division on Mental Retardation and Developmental Disabilities. *Education and Training in Mental Retardation and Developmental Disabilities, 36,* 3–15.

Merriam-Webster Online. (2009a). "Family." Springfield, MA: Merriam-Webster. Retrieved June 21, 2008, from www.merriam-webster.com/dictionary/family

Merriam-Webster Online. (2009b). "Partnership." Springfield, MA: Merriam-Webster. Retrieved June 21, 2008, from www.merriam-webster.com/dictionary/partnership

Murdick, N. L., Gartin, B. C., & Crabtree, T. (2007). *Special education law* (2nd ed.). Upper Saddle River, NJ: Pearson.

National PTA. (1997). *National standards for parent/family involvement programs.* Chicago: Author.

National PTA. (2007). *National standards for family-school partnerships.* Retrieved June 10, 2008, from http://www.pta.org/1216.htm

Newman, L. (2005, September). *Family expectations and involvement for youth with disabilities. NLTS2 Data Brief: Reports from the National Longitudinal Transition Study.* Retrieved July 2, 2008, from www.ncset.org/publications/viewdesc.asp?id=2473

No Child Left Behind Act of 2001, 20 U.S.C. §6301 *et seq.* (2002).

Office of Management and Budget. (2007, December 12). *Program assessment rating tool guidance no. 2007–7.* Retrieved July 9, 2008, from http://www.whitehouse.gov/omb/part/guidance/part_guid_2007-07.pdf

Office of Management and Budget. (2008). *Assessing program performance.* Retrieved July 16, 2008, from http://www.whitehouse.gov/omb/part/index.html

Patton, J. R., & Trainor, A. (2002). Using applied academics to enhance curricular reform in secondary education. In C. Kochhar-Bryant & D. Bassett (Eds.), *Aligning transition and standards-based education: Issues and strategies* (pp. 55–76). Arlington, VA: Council for Exceptional Children.

Pleet, A. (2000). *Investigating the relationship between parent involvement in transition planning and post-school outcomes for students with disabilities.* Michigan: UMI Dissertation Services.

Sheldon, S. B., & Epstein, J. L. (2005). School programs of family and community involvement to support children's reading and literacy development across the grades. In J. Flood & P. Anders (Eds.), *Literacy development of students in urban schools: Research and policy* (pp. 107–138). Newark, DE: International Reading Association.

Storms, J., O'Leary, E., & Williams, J. (2000, May). *The Individuals With Disabilities Education Act of 1997 transition requirements: A guide for states, districts, schools, universities and families: IDEAS that Work.* Washington, DC: U.S. Department of Education Office of Special Education Programs.

Test, D. W., Aspel, N. P., & Everson, J. M. (2006). *Transition methods for youth with disabilities.* Upper Saddle River, NJ: Pearson.

Turnbull, A., Turnbull, R., & Wehmeyer, M. L. (2007). *Exceptional lives: Special education in today's schools* (5th ed.). Upper Saddle River, NJ: Pearson.

Turnbull, R., Huerta, N., & Stowe, M. (2006). *The Individuals With Disabilities Education Act as amended in 2004.* Upper Saddle River, NJ: Pearson.

U.S. Department of Education (2001). *U.S. Department of Education's 1999 performance report and 2001 annual plan.* Retrieved February 18, 2009, from http://www.ed.gov/pubs/AnnualPlan2001/

U.S. Department of Education. (2003). *No Child Left Behind: A parents guide.* Washington, DC: Author. Retrieved July 9, 2008, from http://www.ed.gov/parents/academic/involve/nclbguide/parentsguide.pdf

Wandry, D. L., Webb, K. W., Williams, J. M., Bassett, D. S., Asselin, S. B., & Hutchinson, S. R. (2008). Teacher candidates' perceptions of barriers to effective transition programming. *Career Development for Exceptional Individuals, 31*(1), 14–25.

Wehmeyer, M. L., Palmer, S., Agran, M., Mithaug, D., & Martin, J. (2000). Promoting causal agency: The self-determined learning model of instruction. *Exceptional Children, 66,* 439–453.

Wehmeyer, M. L., Sands, D. J., Knowlton, H. E., & Kozleski, E. B. (2002). *Teaching students with mental retardation: Access to the general curriculum.* Baltimore: Brookes.

Will, M. (1984, March/April). *Bridges from school to working life. Programs for the handicapped.* Washington, DC: Clearinghouse on the Handicapped.

Workforce Investment Act of 1998, 20 U.S.C. § 9201 *et seq.* (1998).

Yell, M. L., & Drasgow, E. (2005). *No Child Left Behind: A guide for professionals.* Upper Saddle River, NJ: Pearson.

ABOUT THE AUTHORS

AMY M. PLEET has over 35 years of experience as an English Teacher, Special Education Teacher, Transition Specialist (district and state department), higher education faculty (Special Education Graduate Director and Associate Professor) and now Secondary Inclusion Consultant with the University of Delaware to districts committed to improving the effectiveness of instruction for included students with disabilities. As the parent of two young adults with disabilities, Dr. Pleet is especially aware of a parent's perspectives and the contributions they can make. Her research and writing focus on building parent partnerships, self-determination, and inclusionary secondary school reform.

DONNA L. WANDRY is an Associate Professor of Special Education at West Chester University of Pennsylvania. Dr. Wandry has served children and youth with disabilities directly in school and agency settings. She was the Project Director for a federal systems change transition grant while serving as the transition coordinator at the Kansas Board of Education, and has taught transition coursework at both the undergraduate and graduate levels in higher education for 15 years. She is a national Past President of the Council for Exceptional Children's Division on Career Development and Transition. Her primary areas of interest are special education legislation and movement from school to adult life for persons with disabilities, with a focus on working with families and providers to create systemic changes that facilitate that movement.

2

Changing Demographics

Vicki A. McGinley

ESSENTIAL QUESTIONS

○ What family characteristics need to be considered in building home–practitioner partnerships?

○ How can practitioners establish practices to address challenges faced by diverse families?

○ How can practitioners establish practices to address challenges diverse families present to them?

○ How can the principles of cultural reciprocity support building relationships with diverse families?

The effect of changing family structure and increasing ethnic/cultural/racial diversity has expanded the complexity of service provision greatly since the passage of the Education for All Handicapped Children Act of 1975, when schools were first required to include parents in the educational planning for students with disabilities. Therefore, the primary focus of this chapter is to describe how changing family structures, including those that are culturally and linguistically diverse (CLD), impact the work of school and adult service professionals as they strive to build partnerships with a wide range of families within the transition planning and implementation process. What are some strategies for building these partnerships?

The explanations and examples relative to family structures and cultural differences cited throughout this chapter are provided to empower practitioners to take the first steps in building cultural reciprocity with parents. They are intended not to limit or stereotype perspectives, but to provide a foundation for practitioners in building a relationship with the individuals with whom they work. Indeed, practitioners are cautioned to avoid stereotyping and assumptions that all families with the same ancestry will relate to them in the same way.

Family Structures

What is family? *Webster's Online Dictionary* defines *family* as (a) a group of individuals living under one roof and usually under one head and (b) the basic unit in society traditionally consisting of two parents rearing their own or adopted children; these options may include any of various social units differing from but regarded as equivalent to the traditional single parent family (Webster's, 2009). These two definitions reflect our changing views of what a family is. Many sociological research studies have studied the configurations of families, reporting diverse models of the family as well as differing responses to parenting a child with disabilities. The predominately two-parent family has been replaced by many family structures, including extended, foster, nuclear, same-sex, single and stepparent models, as seen in the definition above. With each of these models may come a different set of challenges related to child rearing, family functioning, and the interaction between the family and the school or adult agency. Transition processes and challenges are impacted by the changing family structure and diversity in this country.

Understanding Family Challenges

With each family, educators and related professionals will find strengths as well as concerns. It is vital that these practitioners become aware of both. Practitioners need to exhibit sensitivity to the issues the family is facing on a daily basis. Some family systems will face particular challenges more than others will. However, all families may face some of the same challenges:

1. *Stresses of juggling family and work life* that inhibit parenting, individual and couple time, resulting in problems of communication, socialization, and overall well being of family members. At present, the United States is known for long work hours with limited vacation and family leave time. The stress of having a family and working outside of the home may take its toll on how well the family functions. For example, homework may not be done to satisfaction or at all if the parents work late hours and children are spending time at home alone or in other childcare arrangements. This may obviously be less of a problem for a traditional nuclear family where the mother stays home. However, at present, this type of family is the minority. The proportion of all families with married couples in which only the husband was a labor force participant fell from 35% in 1975 to 17% in 2006 (Comartle, 2007). By 2006, according to Comartle, about 7 out of 10 mothers with children under 18 years were labor force participants. Further, of the 3.3 million mothers with children under a year old, 55.1% were in the labor force by 2007 (U.S. Bureau of Labor Statistics, 2008). Stressors of juggling family and work life will certainly impact transition planning and implementation processes as communication among family members, as well as between family members and the school, will be impaired and/or difficult. The toll of long work hours may affect school planning meeting times and attention and follow-through by families.

2. *Conflicts due to missed work* time for school meetings, often exacerbated if their coworkers and supervisors do not have to leave work for child-care responsibilities.

3. *Stresses from poverty,* such as poor housing conditions and nutrition. By 2007, the nation's official poverty rate climbed to 12.5% (U.S. Department of Commerce, 2008). Presently, 18% of children under age 18 live in poverty (U.S. Census Bureau, 2008), further alienating the family from the educational setting as daily survival becomes the families' primary goal. Poor living conditions, as a result of prejudice and poverty, continue to affect a disproportionate number of African Americans. There are major inequities in income, health, and quality of life between African Americans and Anglo Saxon Americans, leaving many families at risk for poor housing, overcrowding, crime, lack of services, high infant mortality, poor health, and psychological problems. Williams (2008) documented that CLD families are less likely to participate in individualized education program (IEP) meetings and transition planning due to poverty, lack of transportation and/or child care, and limited time and resources.

4. *Issues related to having children with serious behavioral and/or medical concerns,* resulting in imbalances in normal family activities. Parents report that frequently their time and energy devoted to a child with serious concerns eclipses family life. In addition to usual parental duties, they spend inordinate amounts of time with specialist appointments and find it difficult to arrange for day care or respite care so that they can have breaks from 24-hour "on-duty" responsibilities. These parents have less energy to devote to educational and transition concerns and may experience a greater sense of parent burnout by the time their children reach adolescence (Murphy, Christian, Caplin, & Young, 2006).

5. *Conflicts arising from family structures.* For example, stepfamilies and grandparents rearing children must deal with roles of family members, issues of boundaries, and conflicts over child rearing. Also, foster families may be dealing with a child's behavioral issues arising from the child being moved about and the reasons behind the placement in foster care in the first place. According to the U.S. Census Bureau (2006) there are 13.6 million single parents in the United States who had custody of 21.2 million children under the age of 21. Single-parent families presently have a higher rate of poverty and the parent, usually the mother, may have to work long hours and rely on outside caregivers. Single females maintain almost 2 in 10 families (Comartle, 2007). Single women maintained 46% of black families and 20% Hispanic or Latino families. Of these households, 28.3% or 4.1 million households were living in poverty. Statistics suggest that CLD families are more likely to be dealing with additional stressors, such as single-parent households and poverty, thus further challenging the transition process and implementation.

Family Diversity

Diversity is defined as (a) differing from one another and (b) composed of distinct or unlike elements or qualities (Webster's, 2009). In addition to the differing family structures described earlier, families also differ based upon the groups with which they are associated. Families living in the United States are likely to be diverse in race, ethnicity, culture, gender, and sexual orientation, as well as in environmental diversity encompassing economic, political, and social conditions (Bialeschki & Pearce, 2007). The demographics of the United States have been rapidly changing and will continue to change in the coming decades to reflect families from many different cultures, ethnicities, races, socioeconomic statuses, and languages. It has been predicted that by mid-21st century, no single ethnic group will make up the majority of the U.S. population. Minorities, now roughly one third of the U.S. population, are expected to become the majority in 2042, with the nation projected to be 54% minority groups in 2050. The Hispanic population is projected to nearly triple, from 46.7 million to 132.8 million during the 2008 to 2050 period. Its share of the nation's population is projected to double, from 15% to 30%. Thus, nearly one in three United States residents will be Hispanic (U.S. Department of Commerce, 2008). The African American population is projected to increase from 41.1 million (14% of the population) in 2008 to 65.7 million (15% of the population) in 2050; the Asian population is projected to climb from 15.5 million (5.1%) to 40 million (9.2%; U.S. Department of Commerce).

According to Hanson (1998), *culture* is the framework that guides one's life. Families from the same cultural background may share tendencies, but not all families who share a common cultural background will behave in the same way. These differences are due to many factors such as socioeconomic status, education, age, religion, location of residence, and the degree of acculturation in this country. When we add in the factor of disability, families may cope and plan differently. Within each diverse family structure and their sociological group, then, there exists the individual family's culture.

Diversity challenges exist for families in which English is not the primary language. These family members may be intimidated by meeting with education and adult service professionals as they may have difficulties understanding technical terminology, special education laws and regulations (Kim & Morningstar, 2005). Also, depending on the cultural background of the family, their value systems may be at odds with the value system of present-day education and adult agencies that currently reflect an Anglo-American value system. According to Geenen, Powers, and Lopez-Vasquez (2001), the institutional and professional structure of the school may be so intimidating to CLD parents that involvement in school-based transition planning may be particularly low overall, and decline during the transition period. Thus, parent support and planning for the transition process as part of the IEP development may be difficult or nonexistent. In fact, families' prior negative experiences with school may be the single most important factor challenging family participation (Geenen et al., 2001).

Challenges Facing Diverse Families During Transition

Building Partnerships With Diverse Families at the Onset of Transition Planning

Families cope with problems across their life spans, but there are additional issues as their children with disabilities approach adolescence. According to Turnbull, Turnbull, and Wehmeyer (2007), families face their most difficult transitional periods during the time of adolescence and entering adulthood. Families confront three specific challenges when children with disabilities enter these transition years: (a) independence versus continued dependence on the family system, (b) issues related to entering the world of work, and (c) sexuality issues. During this time, school and adult service providers must support families as they work with their adolescents in making decisions about instructional goals, including how to address sexuality/gender issues, career preparation choices, independent living skill development, and residential options. For example, in more paternalistic Hispanic families, the fathers may have more difficulty in accepting disability, and thus it may be the mother who interacts more with the school (Garcia, Perez, Ortiz & Alba, 2000). To individualize their services, practitioners will need to know if the family fits into a more paternalistic style of functioning, as this may effect career decisions, as well as interaction style with the family.

Practitioners building partnerships with CLD families need to be sensitive to each family's culture. Decisions continually have to be made regarding which transition areas are most important as well as when, where, and how training and support should be provided. The young adult's preferences must be assessed through these years and matched to the availability of employment, residential options, and social and/or leisure programs. Practitioners must work to find supports and teach the most important skills related to adult independence. At these transition points, schools' and families' views may differ greatly. Geenen and colleagues (2001), interviewed 308 CLD parents regarding their perceived levels of family involved in transition activities; although all participants believed family involvement was important, the CLD families emphasized skills in the home such as personal care, whereas the European American families placed emphasis on school-based transition activities. Some families may be more concerned with socialization and less with moving their child from the family home and into the world of work. For example, members of the Hispanic culture have generally responded to disability by offering support and comfort in the home and community. However, practitioners can view such support as excessive, interfering with the move towards independence for the person with a disability (Cruz, 1979). In the African American family, the extended family has been a source of strength, and group effort for the common interest is taught as a strategy for survival (Billingsley, 1974). This is vastly different from the Euro-American culture, where the concept of family generally refers to immediate family members. Extended family may or may not live close by and may not participate actively in the nuclear family (Lynch & Hanson, 1998). The practitioner must take this level and type of involvement, as well as tim-ing (age of child with disability), into consideration.

Because transition planning is about adult life, educators must fully explore with youth and parents their expectations and vision, both short- and long-term, to ensure their child's participation in all facets of adult activity. In addition, practitioners must help parents identify the kinds of support that will be needed (Turnbull, Turnbull, Bronicki, Summers, & Roerder-Gorder, 1989).

Challenges Diverse Families Face When Children With Disabilities Enter Adulthood

Some of the same challenges faced by the family of an adolescent with disabilities during high school will continue into adulthood, but may now become exacerbated as siblings who once were a support leave the home and parents age. Adult service providers are confronted with providing services to families that may hold different belief systems about disability. As a result, practitioners may cause offense with differences in expectations related to self-determination, independence, and community participation (Kim & Morningstar, 2005). In some families, children have little or no authority to make decisions and if a discrepancy exists between parent and child, the parent's expectations prevail (Kalyanpur, Harry, & Skrtic, 2000). Adult service providers also need to provide services to families who handle life stresses such as finances, work, aging, and success differently, and have to vary their services depending on the family dynamics. Kuehn and Imm-Thomas (1993) outlined an example of these challenges; they reported that Native Americans had a disproportionately high incidence of disability and high rates of unemployment. However, although Native Americans are in high need of adult services, the traditional organized and delivered rehabilitation programs have been largely unsuccessful with this population. Martin, Frank, Minkler, and Johnson's survey (1988) of vocational rehabilitation counselors who worked with Native Americans found that the counselors considered sensitivity to culture (including language and community) the most effective approach to working with these families. Knowing the value system of different cultural groups around issues of the life stresses mentioned above will help the adult service provider in working with the family.

Joe (1988) found that the remoteness of the family residence related to whether or not parents referred their sons and daughters for disability related services. A reluctance to use services and problems faced by minorities with disabilities are exacerbated by the social inequities of having multiple minority status. This has been found with the Latino population in particular, as they have to cope with ethnic, racial, linguistic and disability inequities (Arnold, 1983).

In addition, Baldwin and Smith (1984) reported that adult services, particularly rehabilitation in the United States, can be a very selective process whereby only individuals identified as being "most likely to succeed" receive the services, as those persons with disabilities may be easier to work with. Thus, minorities with disabilities have an even greater hurdle to cross as data support that African American and Hispanic American youth with disabilities have greater difficulty than Euro American youth with disabilities finding employment (Blackorby & Wagner, 1996) and do not appear to have equal access to vocational rehabilitation services.

Cultural Reciprocity as a Framework

Deepening Cultural Sensitivity

Persons working with children (e.g., educators, counselors, therapists, adult service providers) need to have a sense of how the structure and diversity of the individual family may affect school planning, particularly planning for transitioning the student from school to adult roles. According to Diken (2006), a family's culture and ethnic group influences the response of a family to disability. Individuals from within these families may treat disability differently depending on family structure, gender, and beliefs about health and acculturation. Researchers who have studied Hispanic culture's beliefs about the nature of disability have found that this population may interpret disability as divine punishment, and some within this group may seek the help of a folk healer (Seligman & Darling, 2007; Spector, 1985). Families of Native American ancestry may view causation of disability as witchcraft, spirit loss, or taboo actions, and turn to tribal ceremonies to help the family and the child (Seligman & Darling). Families with Anglo European backgrounds generally believe in scientific causes for disability, including genetics, environmental agents, and disease, as well as prenatal and perinatal stress. In the African American community, disability may be interpreted in one of two ways: as bad luck or misfortune, and, less so, as the result of the father (Willis, 1992). Among various Asian ethnic groups, the most severe disabling conditions (i.e., those associated with developmental disabilities) are traditionally viewed with considerable stigma. Causation of disability may focus on the mother's presumed failure to follow prescribed dietary and other health care regiments or her violation of some taboo. Illnesses may be attributed to either external or internal forces such as excessive emotions of joy, anger, hate, jealousy, sorrow, worry, or fear (Chan, 1992). Other Asian Americans, such as those from Korean backgrounds, have been influenced by the above-mentioned religions as well as by Shamanism (Chan). In this religion, according to Mun (1979), the spirit must be worshipped and well served to prevent misfortune (i.e., disability) and to bring good fortune. Knowing the family's belief system about the origin of disability may help the adult service provider to understand the decisions being made by the family and help identify what kind of supports are needed in working with the family.

Cultural Reciprocity as a Gateway to Collaboration

According to Kalyanpur and Harry (1999), there are three levels of cultural awareness: overt, covert, and subtle. Although all three levels of cultural awareness are important in developing reciprocal relationships with families, professionals who employ the subtle level of awareness on a regular basis in their practice may be more effective with diverse families. The *overt level* refers to awareness of obvious external differences, such as manner of dress and language spoken. Practitioners operating at this level of awareness may fall into the trap of assuming that all families with a given cultural background are the same. They may interact with the family from these stereotyped misconceptions, which are likely to limit the development of a partnership with that family.

Practitioners move to the *covert level* of awareness when they begin to observe individual differences that this family may exhibit, such as communication style or response to professionals that reflect their values about status. For instance, a practitioner may note that a family tends to remain silent during part of a planning meeting. The practitioner may not be able to tell whether the family's silence reflects agreement or not, but may choose to proceed with the meeting under the assumption that the family concurs. When operating at the covert level of awareness, however, the professional will seek the family's explanation for this silence. In order for practitioners to operate at the covert level, they must have a background of knowledge about the specific cultural group. Specific knowledge about a cultural group tends to be stereotypic and not always helpful. Acculturation levels of families vary greatly, affecting how closely they conform to these expectations of behavior. However, practitioners who do not move beyond the covert level will not truly build meaningful partnerships with families.

The *subtle level* of cultural awareness involves awareness of the beliefs and values that the family holds that may be in contrast with those embedded in our disability systems. To achieve this level of awareness, Kalyanpur and Harry (1999) advise practitioners to ask themselves "Why?" (e.g., "Why do I want 21-year-old Hussein to move out on his own into a group home?," p. 117). By posing this question, the involved practitioner begins to understand that the special education culture values independence and self-reliance. Hussein's family may value interdependence and might not agree that he should leave the family home, particularly as none of his nondisabled siblings did so either. Only by becoming aware of the values embedded within the disability system and then openly seeking to understand the family's values can subtle "cultural dissonance" be detected and addressed.

Strategies for Using Cultural Reciprocity to Build Partnerships With Diverse Families

The teaching profession continues to be composed primarily of white women of Anglo-European origins. This lack of diversity in the profession means that few teachers have had the opportunity to learn about diverse cultural and linguistic groups through peer or professional relationships, either as they themselves went through school or in the schools in which they are employed (Thorp, 1997). Recently, higher education institutions have begun embedding competencies related to working with diverse populations in preservice training programs. Specifically, accredited educational programs are expected to clearly articulate proficiencies related to diversity in their conceptual framework, delineating knowledge and skills that candidates are expected to develop during their professional programs through curriculum and field experiences that provide a well-grounded framework for understanding diversity, including English language learners and students with exceptionalities (National Council for Accreditation of Teacher Education, 2008).

Those professionals already working with families require ongoing training and exposure to culturally and linguistically diverse populations. Actively including diverse people in trainings and meetings, providing services in the family's native language directly in their community, and developing employment in the family's own community have been found to be most successful in working with diverse families (Zhang, 2003). In addition, practitioners need to develop a thorough understanding of cultural influences; sensitivity to the similarities and differences between themselves and the families they serve may help in the transition process (Gladding, 1998). According to Kim and Morningstar (2005), after explicit discussion with families regarding cultural values and practices, professionals should make their best effort to establish mutual goals that are acceptable to both the professional's and to the family's values.

Kalyanpur and Harry (1999) introduced the concept of *cultural reciprocity* with a framework for building better understanding of the culture in our educational and adult service systems in contrast to the cultures of the families who are served. Their work promotes an awareness of the underlying values of the system as well as an understanding of the values of the families, which serves to avoid stereotyping. They recommend a four-step process to build cultural reciprocity:

1. *The professional will reflect on their own values and reactions and those of the organization they represent.* This step is not as easy as it sounds as we often don't recognize how acclimated we are to the values of our disability system until we encounter someone who comes from a different orientation. Values are embedded not only in the professional interpretation of the student's difficulties, but also underpin recommendations for service. This step also involves exploring attitudes about disability, as well recognition of the powerful role of professionals (Thorp, 1997).

2. *The professional will investigate the values of the family,* beginning with the overt generalizations that are known about people from that culture, but going beyond the instinct to stereotype to discover the covert and subtle values of that individual family. Additionally, professionals must find out about the community in which the family lives so as to gain knowledge about resources, what families do, and where they go. Professionals must keep in mind that each family is unique in its cultural beliefs. To what extent does the family accept the assumptions and values inherent in the professional interpretation of the youth's disability and recommendations for programming and service?

3. *The professional will iterate the distinction between the two sets of values.* Only by openly stating and respecting the differences can they be recognized and discussed. It is the professional's responsibility to explain the disability, cultural variables within the diagnostic process, and recommendations to set the tone for further discussion.

4. *The professional will work collaboratively with the family to come to a resolution* that respects the values of all parties. Once there is understanding of the differences in values, alternative approaches to the youth's needs may be considered.

Conclusion

In developing partnerships with families of youth with disabilities, practitioners should consider the uniqueness, strengths, and challenges each family brings to the transition planning process. It's important to work to understand families' communication styles, their level of comfort in involvement with educational professionals, and the degree of involvement that is appropriate for each individual family. Some families may welcome the participation of extended family members and/or community members in meetings relating to the youth's services. Practitioners can build cultural reciprocity by first identifying the values embedded in the disability system and then encouraging the family to share their values and beliefs. Open discussion of differences of critical importance can lead to partnerships that will develop flexible solutions all parties will own. Ultimately, youth with disabilities will be the ones to benefit from a united support network as they strive for successful adult outcomes.

INDICATORS OF SUCCESS FOR PARTNERSHIPS THAT ARE SENSITIVE TO DIVERSE FAMILIES

○ Culturally and linguistically diverse families are welcomed to participate in their child's education as well as at the systems level.

○ The school or agency provides supports to the practitioners in building their proficiency in working with diverse families.

○ Culturally appropriate supports are available to families.

○ Practitioners employ the principles of cultural reciprocity in identifying and resolving cultural differences.

REFERENCES

Arnold, B. R. (1983). Attitudinal research and the Hispanic handicapped: A review of selected needs. *Journal of Rehabilitation, 49*, 36–38.

Baldwin, C. H., & Smith, R. T. (1984). An evaluation of the referral and rehabilitation process among the minority handicapped. *International Journal of Rehabilitation Research, 7*, 299–315.

Bialeschki, M., & Pearce, K. (2007). "I don't want a lifestyle—I want a life": The effects of role negotiations on the leisure of lesbian mothers. *Journal of Leisure Research, 29*(1), 113–131.

Billingsley, A. (1974). *Black families and the struggle for survival: Teaching our children to walk tall.* New York: Friendship Press.

Blackorby, J., & Wagner, M. (1996). Longitudinal post-school outcomes of youth with disabilities: Findings from The National Longitudinal Transition Study. *Exceptional Children, 62*, 399–413.

Chan, S. (1992). Ethnic, cultural, and language diversity in intervention settings. In E. W. Lynch and M. J. Hanson (Eds.), *Developing cross-cultural competence: A guide for working with young children and their families* (pp. 181–250). Baltimore: Paul H. Brookes.

Comartle, S. (2007). Labor force status: A visual essay. *Monthly Labor Review, 130*(7), 35–41.

Cruz, D. (1979). Outreach problems in Puerto Rico. In G. Dixon & C. Bridges (Eds.), *On being Hispanic and disabled: The special challenges of an underserved population.* Washington, DC: Partners of Americans.

Diken, I. H. (2006). An overview of parental perceptions in cross-cultural groups on disability. *Childhood Education, 82,* 236–240.

Garcia, S. B., Perez, A., Ortiz, A., & Alba, A. (2000). Mexican American mothers' beliefs about disabilities: Implications for early childhood intervention. *Remedial and Special Education, 21,* 90–102.

Geenen, S., Powers, L. E., & Lopez-Vasquez, A. (2001). Multicultural aspects of parent involvement in transition planning. *Exceptional Children, 67,* 265–282.

Gladding, S. (1998). *Family therapy: History, theory, and practice* (2nd ed.). Upper Saddle River, NJ: Prentice Hall.

Hanson, M. J. (1998). Ethnic, cultural, and language diversity in intervention settings. In E. W. Lynch and M. J. Hanson (Eds.), *Developing cross-cultural competence: A guide for working with young children and their families* (pp. 3–18). Baltimore: Paul H. Brookes.

Joe, J. R. (1988). Government policies and disabled people in American Indian communities. *Disability, Handicap and Society, 3,* 253–262.

Kalyanpur, M., & Harry, B. (1999). *Culture in special education: Building reciprocal family–professional relationships.* Baltimore: Paul H. Brookes.

Kalyanpur, M., Harry, B., & Skrtic, T. (2000). Equity and advocacy expectations of culturally diverse families' participation in special education. *International Journal of Disability, Development and Education, 47,* 119–136.

Kim, K., & Morningstar, M. (2005). Transition planning involving culturally and linguistically diverse families. *Career Development for Exceptional Individuals, 28,* 92–103.

Kuehn, M. L., & Imm-Thomas, P. (1993). A multicultural context. In E. Sutton, A. R. Factor, B. A. Hawkins, T. Heller, & G. B. Seltzer (Eds.), *Older adults with developmental disabilities: Optimizing choice and change* (pp. 327–343). Baltimore: Paul H. Brookes.

Lynch E. W., & Hanson, M. J. (1998). *Developing cross-cultural competence: A guide for working with young children and their families.* Baltimore: Paul H. Brookes.

Martin, W. E., Frank, L. W., Minkler, S., & Johnson, M. (1988). A survey of vocational rehabilitation counselors who work with older American Indians who are visually impaired. *American Rehabilitation, 19*(1), 2–6, 37.

Mun, S. H. (1979). Shamanism in Korea. In Y. C. Shin (Ed.), *Korean thoughts* (pp. 17–36). Seoul, Korea: International Cultural Foundation.

Murphy, N. A., Christian, D. B., Caplin, D. A., & Young, P. C. (2006). The health of caregivers for children with disabilities: Caregiver perspectives. *Child Care Health and Development, 33,* 180–187.

National Council for Accreditation of Teacher Education. (2008). *NCATE unit standards.* Retrieved January 1, 2009, from http://www.ncate.org/public/unitStandardsRubrics.asp?ch=4#stnd4

Seligman, M., & Darling, R. (2007). *Ordinary families: Special children.* New York: Guilford.

Spector, R. E. (1985). *Cultural diversity in health and illness.* New York: Appleton-Century-Crofts.

Thorp, E. (1997). Increasing opportunities for partnership with culturally and linguistically diverse families. *Intervention in the School and Clinic, 3,* 261–270.

Turnbull, H. R., Turnbull, A. P., Bronicki, G. J., Summers, J. A., & Roerder-Gordon, C. (1989). *Disability and the family: A guide to decisions for adulthood.* Baltimore: Paul H. Brookes.

Turnbull, H. R., Turnbull, A. P., & Wehmeyer, M. L. (2007). *Exceptional lives: Special education in today's schools* (5th ed.). Upper Saddle River, NJ: Pearson.

U.S. Bureau of Labor Statistics. (2008, May). *Employment characteristics of families in 2007.* Economic News Release. Retrieved November 15, 2008, from http://www.bls.gov/news.release/famee.nr0.htm.

U.S. Census Bureau. (2006). *Household relationship and living arrangement of children under 18 years of age, sex, race, and Hispanic origin.* Retrieved November 16, 2008, from http://www.census.gov/population/socdemo/hh-fam/cps2006/tabC2-all.csv

U.S. Census Bureau. (2008). Poverty rates by age: 1959 to 2007. Current Populations Survey, 1960 to 2008 Annual Social and Economic Supplements. Retrieved November 16, 2008, from http://www.census.gov/apsd/techdoc/cps/cpsmar07.pdf

U.S. Department of Commerce. (2008, August). *An older and more diverse nation by mid-century.* Retrieved November 16, 2008, from http://www.census.gov/press-release/www/releases/archives/population/012496.html

Webster's Online Dictionary. (2009). Available: http://www.websters-online-dictionary.org

Williams, T. (2008, March). *Transition planning for culturally and linguistically diverse (CLD) families of youth with disabilities: Issues and trends.* Powerpoint presentation handouts for the Summer Transition Institute, University of Kansas, Lawrence. Available http://transitioncoalition.org/transitin/file.php?path=files.docs/CLD_Summer_Institute_08ppt1214341047.ppt

Willis, W. (1992). Ethnic, cultural, and language diversity in intervention settings. In E. W. Lynch and M. J. Hanson (Eds.), *Developing cross-cultural competence: A guide for working with young children and their families* (pp. 121–146). Baltimore: Paul H. Brookes.

Zhang, C. (2003). Facilitating the meaningful participation of culturally and linguistically diverse families in the IFSP and IEP process. *Focus on Autism and Other Developmental Disabilities, 18,* 51–59.

ABOUT THE AUTHOR

VICKI A. MCGINLEY is currently a Professor of Special Education at West Chester University. Her interests are in the areas of communication and behavior disorders, inclusive classrooms and communities, legal issues in education, and urban education. Dr. McGinley serves as a state hearing officer and has served as an educational mediator.

3

Parents as Collaborators

Building Partnerships With School- and Community-Based Providers

Sharon deFur

ESSENTIAL QUESTIONS

○ What are the qualities of effective family/practitioner partnerships?

○ What are the opportunities and challenges within school and agency structures to build collaborative partnerships with families?

Parental involvement and parent–school–community partnerships receive wide acclaim for making a positive difference in the educational and transition outcomes for youth with and without disabilities (Epstein, 2005; Family Strengthening Policy Center, 2004; Harvard Family Research Project, 2007; Lindstrom, Doren, Metheny, Johnson, & Zane, 2007; Wood, Rogers, & Yancey, 2006). Although the impact of parental involvement in education remains undisputed, secondary education traditionally emphasizes the emerging adult independence of adolescents as developmentally appropriate. Consequently, the role of parents in secondary education often receives diminished attention. For example, participation in student individualized education program (IEP) meetings, attendance at optional parent–teacher conferences, back-to-school night meetings, or other traditional family involvement indices frequently decrease during high school (Harvard Family Research Project, 2007).

At the same time, the majority of families, with and without children with disabilities, take for granted that there will be a lifetime relationship among family members. Some families presume this care-giving responsibility relationship extends to all members of the family. Adopting a family-collaboration perspective, the transition field must recognize that families continue to influence and support their children with disabilities well into adulthood, and that seeking adult independence for young adults with disabilities while establishing interdependence with families is not a contradictory strategy. In fact, partnerships between parents and service providers during the transition period represent a critical strategy toward achieving student transition goals. Partnerships between families and transition service providers serve two primary purposes: (a) to improve transition services and outcomes for youth with disabilities, and (b) to develop within each family the knowledge and skills that will be needed for families to continue in an appropriate support role for their adult son or daughter with a disability.

Developing School-Based, Community-Based, and Family Partnerships

Partnerships require intentional development. When we imagine successful partners (whether they are singers, athletes, dancers, business partners, etc.), we assume that these individuals devoted time preparing for their role as partner. Although youth and young adults with disabilities and their families may have been participating with the special education system for many years, there is no guarantee that these years of participation resulted in a commitment to a collaborative partnership. In truth, it is unlikely that many educators and families engaged in conversations regarding postschool expectations or plans prior to the legislative requirement to do so at or prior to the mandated age of 16. Martin, Marshall, and Sale (2004) suggest that early implementers of the Education of All Handicapped Children Act of 1975 were possibly even skeptics of family involvement in developing educational programs for children and youth with disabilities. Undoubtedly, this authoritarian attitude influenced subsequent years of transition planning. Service providers, youth with disabilities, and parents continue to experience uncertainty in how to best collaborate while planning for postsecondary goals and transition services for youth with disabilities.

What Is a Partnership?

Partners define roles and responsibilities and they hold themselves and one another accountable for carrying out responsibilities (see box, "What Is a Partnership?"). This definition of what it means to partner, combined with the research on family and service provider collaboration (Blue-Banning, Summers, Frankland, Nelson, & Beegle, 2004; deFur, 2003; deFur, Todd-Allen, & Getzel, 2001; Knight, 2002), provides the basis for a family partnership model (see Figure 1) for transition planning and services. The model is organized around 10 strategies that contribute to collaborative transition partnerships:

1. Staying student- and family-centered throughout the transition process.
2. Developing a shared vision for student transition outcomes.

WHAT IS A PARTNERSHIP?

- Have a joint interest—partners hold a common vision and set clear goals.

- Play on the same side—partners communicate honestly and openly, sharing and seeking information; they learn from one another; they use one another's strengths and help compensate for one another's limitations.

- Engage in activities to achieve a common goal—partners share responsibilities and trust one another in carrying out those activities.

- Reinforce one another—partners support one another's efforts; they fill in for one another as appropriate to their respective skills.

- Share a common vocabulary or language that promotes understanding of their joint interest—partners use jargon-free speech.

- Share power and decision making—partners recognize one another's perspectives and opinions as valid and consider them in making decisions.

- Share successes—partners credit the partnership as well as themselves.

- Share risks—partners believe that no one person is to blame when failures occur.

- Solve problems jointly—partners engage in active problem solving together.

3. Being culturally responsive and recognizing that families, students, and service providers have complementary expertise to contribute to the transition process.
4. Communicating proactively.
5. Being caring and committed.
6. Giving choice and voice to all parties involved in the transition process.
7. Facilitating creative problem solving to implement effective transition services.
8. Offering helpful connections for families and students during the transition years.
9. Taking action on decisions regarding transition services.
10. Reflecting on and celebrating accomplishments during the transition process.

In isolation, each strategy offers an opportunity to improve the quality of partnerships with families. Taken together, these 10 strategies create a model for collaborating with families that promises to produce positive transition outcomes for youths and young adults with disabilities.

Be Student- and Family-Centered

There is a need to dispel the myth that youth with disabilities and their parents are inherently in conflict. Based on the National Longitudinal

FIGURE 1: Family Partnership Model

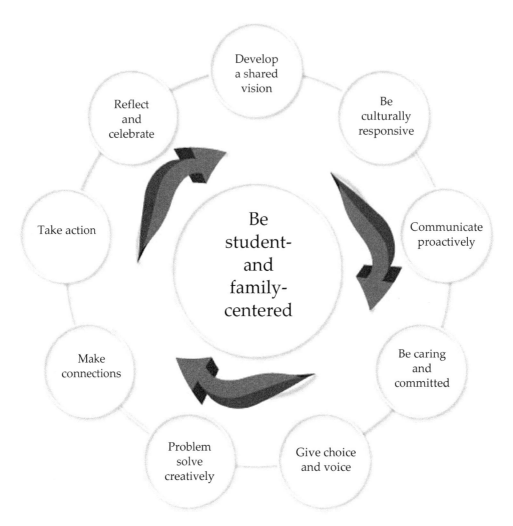

Transition Study 2 (NTLS2), Wagner, Newman, Cameto, Levine, and Marder (2007) report that youth with disabilities say they have strong, positive relationships with their parents and that parents are the first people these youth turn to for support. Student-centered transition planning must also be family-centered transition planning.

The 1990 Individuals With Disabilities Education Act (IDEA) legislation established the requirement to invite students with disabilities to participate in their IEP whenever transition services are discussed. The Individuals With Disabilities Education Improvement Act of 2004 (IDEA, 2004) established that transition must be addressed by the age of 16 (some states have kept age 14 consistent with the 1997 IDEA regulations). To ensure that the IEP reflects student needs, interests, and preferences, student input must be obtained even if students choose not to, or are unable to, attend. Families must be advised prior to the IEP meeting that transition planning is a purpose of the meeting, and that the student will be invited. Parents and students are equal participants in the IEP decision-making process. Clearly, the IDEA 2004 legislation (§ 300.43) intended a strengths-based approach; it reiterates that transition services must be based on an assessment of student strengths as well as needs, interests and preferences.

In spite of an almost 35-year history of family participation in IEP meetings and nearly 20 years of inviting youths as participants, family and student involvement in this critical decision-making process, particularly during the transition years, remains elusive. The regulations governing IEPs have always stated that the child could be included in the IEP meeting when appropriate; however, prior to the 1992 IDEA regulations student participation was very rare. Actual attendance at IEP meetings by youth, now a mandate, is a more frequent occurrence in this era. Still, families and students express concerns that they do not understand the purpose of the IEP transition meeting. Families often report that the IEP transition meeting focuses on student deficits. Unfortunately, when parents and students attend the transition IEP, their participation in the transition planning process is often described as passive (Collet-Klingenberg, 1998; Hasazi, Furney, & Destefano, 1999; Martin et al., 2004; Powers, Turner, Matuszewski, Wilson, & Loesch, 1999; Thoma, Rogan, & Baker, 2001; Zhang & Stecker, 2001). Varying reasons explain this lack of active participation at IEP transition planning meetings. For both parents and students, barriers include: (a) the use of educational jargon by service providers (deFur et al., 2001; Harry, 2008; Harry, Allen, & McLaughlin, 1995; Powers et al.; Thoma et al.); (b) gaps in student and parent knowledge about the process and the available options for transition services (Collet-Klingenberg, 1998); (c) a failure to create a welcoming environment or to seek input from students and families (deFur et al.; Powers et al.); and, (d) the perception that meetings are professionally driven, document focused, time-limited, and structured based on professional and compliance needs (deFur et al.; Harry).

> ❝ Let me talk about the joy [sic] of going to Tim's IEP meeting . . . after IEP meeting . . . after IEP meeting . . ., where I was regularly handed thick papers and then asked to sign on the dotted line that I understood my rights. . . . This policy was then followed by the IEP team [sic] decisions that were made about my son's high school transition course of studies. ❞
>
> *A mother of a student receiving special education services*

Martin and colleagues (2004) collected posttransition IEP meeting surveys from 1,689 participants including parents, students, special and general educators, administrators, and related service providers. Students responded to the surveys in ways that indicated that they did not know the reasons for the IEP transition meeting, did not understand what was said at the meetings, and did not know what they needed to do next. These researchers also learned that students were somewhat uncomfortable in offering ideas or recommendations regarding the IEP transition plan. In spite of this, Martin et al. found that when students attended, parents reported understanding the reason for the meeting at significantly higher rates than when students did not attend. Student presence also resulted in parents agreeing that they understood the conversation of the IEP meeting and that they, as parents, knew what to expect or do next. According to Martin et al., student presence at the meeting even resulted in greater participation by general educators, related service providers, and administrators and increased focus on student strengths. One might suggest that being student-centered transforms participant perceptions.

Hasazi et al. (1999) found that localities that were successful in involving students and families took proactive steps to prepare students and families to be active participants in the transition planning IEP process. They suggested that student participation in the IEP meeting worked best when students understood their disability, the IEP process, the terminology, and had practiced meeting skills prior to the IEP meeting. Further, a student-centered transition planning process used student participation in the IEP as an opportunity to develop and demonstrate skills of self-determination. Powers et al. (1999) found unanimous support for student involvement in transition planning despite reported challenges for students, families, and educators. Martin et al. (2004) remind the field that when students attend their IEP without preparation—where they do not know what to do, do not understand the goals or purpose of the meeting, or feel like no one listens to them when they do talk—they could decide that attending the IEP meeting is a meaningless activity. Martin and colleagues go so far as to suggest that this practice may actually be harmful.

To meet the intent of the law means that service providers must be student- and family-centered. Service providers must take the time to educate and prepare youth and families about the transition planning process, including how to participate in the IEP transition meeting. Among the variety of strategies to enhance this process (e.g., Arndt, Konrad, & Test, 2006; Hammer, 2004; McGahee-Kovac, 2002), service providers might encourage students and families to bring another person along with them to the IEP meeting to help them discern the discussion and the decisions. Other welcoming steps (as appropriate) include the arrangements of the space and a clear agenda describing the process; nametags; notepads; and refreshments. Asking students and family members to tell their own stories about the successes students are having, or challenges they are facing presents an opportunity for students and families for students and families to assume their partner role.

INDICATORS OF SUCCESS FOR FAMILY-CENTERED TRANSITION PLANNING

- ○ Students and family members actively participate in the transition planning process, engaging in the dialogue and the decision making.
- ○ The IEP transition meeting process facilitates participation by students and family members.
- ○ Families or students bring a friend or a relative to the meeting to provide support when needed.
- ○ Students and family members are satisfied with the process and the content of the IEP transition planning meeting.

Develop a Shared Vision

A clear articulation of a future vision for the child or youth with a disability has been missing from the traditional IEP process, and to some degree from the transition mandates. That is, no federal policy mandates this step nor does such policy describe the IEP as a long-term strategic plan. Yet student-centered planning that begins with a shared and articulated vision based on student and family needs and interests receives support from professionals and families who regard that vision as critical to a quality transition plan (deFur, 2003; Schwartz, Jacobson, & Holburn, 2000; Storms, O'Leary, & Williams, 2000). Beginning the IEP transition planning process with a focus on the family and student's vision orients all IEP team members to the true purpose of the meeting. It provides a clear venue for family and student leadership and input and creates a shared vision, a necessity for effective team actions. Student transition assessment that grounds the students, parents, and service providers in the reality of the possible and the positive makes the vision both realistic and attainable.

> ❝ When J came to his first high school IEP meeting, his goals for courses and graduation were low . . . . Each year he participated more, and now he says he wants to go to college and take advanced classes. He was willing to go to summer school to catch up. [Tearfully] And now he has been accepted at college . . . . His teacher helped him be a leader in his IEP and now he is speaking out in IEP meetings and his school is responding. ❞
>
> *A mother of a high school student*

Unquestionably, the increased emphasis on academic standards may seem to force some students and their families to focus their vision to choose between two courses of study. The choice may be between a primary focus on occupational preparation in high school and a course of study that meets the academic expectations of applying for postsecondary education. In reality, most jobs of the future will require some postsecondary training or education. Parent encouragement to pursue additional schooling post-high school has a strong influence on a young adult's decision. Public schools are held accountable for providing an educational program that supports students' academic goals, including postsecondary education, which is a required area for discussion in the transition IEP. Under the No Child Left Behind Act of 2001, parents can actually exercise their right for school choice if their child's current school fails to make annual yearly progress (AYP) for 2 years in a row (20 U.S.C. § 6316 (b)(1)(E)(i)). Families can choose to have their child transfer to another high school in the district that did make AYP and that student can remain in that school until he or she graduates. If there is no other school in the district, the school board may enter into an agreement with a neighboring school district to make other choice options available to the family. The dilemma is that 75% of America's school districts have only one high school (Alliance for Excellent Education, 2007), thus limiting school choice options.

Some in the transition field expressed concerns that reauthorization of the Individuals With Disabilities Education Improvement Act in 2004 deemphasized the focus on transition. Countering this concern is the fact that transition and transition outcomes have become primary accountability measures for the special education that students receive in public schools. For example, IDEA 2004 (Section 616) requires states to develop and report on performance measures that operationally describe the effectiveness of special education for students in that state. States must develop performance indicators and report on: (a) the percentage of youth aged 16 and above with an IEP that includes coordinated, measurable, annual IEP goals and transition services that will reasonably enable the student to meet his postsecondary goals; and (b) the percentage of youth who had IEPs, are no longer in secondary school, and who have been competitively employed, enrolled in some type of postsecondary school, or both, within 1 year of leaving high school. States must also report on graduation rates and on drop-out rates. States, and consequently, local districts, are evaluated using performance measures linked to these transition outcomes.

An unspoken expectation of both policy and policy makers is that schools prepare students for successful transitions with readiness to achieve their postsecondary goals. With a shared vision for the future, families and service providers can work together to improve student academic achievement and to create IEPs that exert "holding" power to keep students invested and involved in schools. Developing a course of study with an action plan for transition activities that is revisited and revised each year provides a picture of what has been accomplished and what needs to be accomplished to achieve long-term goals. Transition services should include strategies to make schools more personal, to raise academic expectations, and to improve a student's basic literacy and numeracy skills as well as develop plans for a future career and living independently. Keeping the vision in the forefront reminds students, families, and service providers of the reason for school-based transition services.

INDICATORS OF SUCCESS FOR A SHARED VISION FOR TRANSITION

○ Service providers and families hold high, appropriate expectations for youth success.

○ Planning begins with a discussion of the student's strengths, interests, and needs based on transition assessment; the IEP team develops a shared vision for the student's future and documents it in the IEP.

○ Students and their families discuss long-term goals and the steps that students, families, and schools must take to achieve these goals.

○ Families help develop the youth's course of study and transition activities within the context of the shared vision.

○ Students, families, and service providers recognize that long-term transition goals may change or be reframed as students experience their secondary school life.

○ The family is increasingly engaged in the student's secondary education.

Be Culturally Responsive

No partnership can develop or grow stronger without trust. Blue-Banning et al. (2004) describes a trusting relationship between school and parents as being one where each of the members sees the others as dependable and honest while honoring the discreteness needed when stories are shared. Trust comes when parent and school collaborators respect one another, avoid being judgmental, and demonstrate that they value the youth with a disability. We develop trust more readily when we listen to and try to understand each other's stories, each other's culture, and our own selves. Transition service providers must engage in practices that develop and strengthen our cultural responsiveness. Harry (2008) challenges the field that if we are to be successful in developing trust with many of the families of youth with disabilities, then we have to be willing to examine our position as culturally responsive service providers.

The last United States Census data (2000) confirmed the shifting demographics of the country from that of primarily Anglo-Saxon with an African American minority to a country with increasing numbers of families of Hispanic origin from all over the world and increasing numbers of families from Asia with varied ethnic and cultural backgrounds. Immigration from Eastern Europe, South America, and Africa also continues to change the face of America. In the next 2 decades, many communities will experience a shift to a multiethnic and mixed race population. In contrast, most educators and service providers do not reflect these demographics nor have they had the cultural experiences that offer them a perspective different from their own.

Differing values, attitudes, and priorities develop within these cultural contexts. For example, not all cultures share a future orientation; in fact, this is a minority view among the world's 6 billion humans. The typical U.S. citizen presumes equality between individuals and expects eye contact and self-assurance; this violates many cultural traditions. Our American work ethic puts a high premium on "doing things"—being pragmatic—at the expense of "being and becoming" (Hodgkinson, 2000). The interpretation of disability and its relationship to strengths and needs may vary based on culture. For instance, the very conversation that transition service providers seek to have about future planning, self-determination, strengths and needs, and productive adult lives may contradict the expectations and experience of families with whom we wish to partner. In addition to country of origin, every family and service provider exists within their own ecological context, differing in economic means, family systems, heritage, and education. All of these factors create potential for cultural collision.

> If schools are to create environments that enable youths to be themselves, as well as help find a "fitting place" in society, the old procedure of requiring youth to "leave their culture and language at the schoolhouse door" must be discarded.
>
> *A mother*

Gil-Kashiabara, Hogansen, Geenen, Powers, and Powers (2007) interviewed parents of high school youth, two thirds of whom were from non-Anglo backgrounds. They found that these parents were not familiar with transition planning or the legal requirements of transition planning. Barriers to their participation in transition planning included work-related barriers (e.g., time off from work), communication barriers (e.g., notification, language differences, etc.), and personal barriers (e.g., feelings of inadequate preparation). These cultural contexts must be considered as our partnerships develop.

In reality, each of us is ethnocentric; that is, both families and service providers see and interpret interactions and take action based on their own cultural filter. Strength exists within this diversity of thought and opinions, but so does the potential for conflict and misunderstanding as most people have limited direct experiences with people from different culture and family contexts. Developing cultural responsiveness requires that practitioners examine their own values, beliefs, and attitudes and develop the skills of suspending judgment and of respecting the diversity of the families with whom they work. Service providers must become educated in the cultural beliefs of the families whose children they serve, including for some the role of extended family or community family (Harvard Family Research Project, 2007). We can begin by inviting and listening to the stories of families, learning from families, and recognizing the complementary expertise families bring to the transition process.

INDICATORS OF SUCCESS FOR CULTURAL RESPONSIVENESS

○ Service providers ask families about their language of preference and their cultural traditions with the goal of respecting each family's unique traditions.

○ Service providers arrange meetings that include family decision makers and occur at times and places that respect family cultural traditions and ecological context.

○ Service providers recognize that each family's culture is unique, regardless of racial, economic, or ethnic heritage.

○ Families share ways in which they are assisting their son or daughter to develop independence within their family and community.

○ Practitioners are aware of their own ethnocentricity and attitudes toward other cultural, racial, ethnic, and socioeconomic groups and develop skills of suspending those attitudes

Communicate Proactively

Parents value transition service providers who provide concrete and accessible information about transition services within the school and community setting. They appreciate not having to ask for information—particularly during this transition period, when they are not sure what to ask for. They rely on service providers to teach them about the transition process and the transition service system, and see the family's role as teaching the service provider about the youth or young adult with a disability. Families want a sufficient quantity of information that enables efficient and effective coordination and understanding among the partners as well as quality information where the communication is positive, understandable, and respectful at all levels of the partnership (Blue-Banning et al. 2004; deFur et al., 2001; Hanley-Maxwell, Pogoloff, & Whitney-Thomas, 1998; Wehmeyer, Morningstar, & Husted, 1999).

Communication involves both giving information and receiving feedback; it is not finished when the information is just given. Transition service providers believe that they communicate frequently with families; that is, they call, they send letters, or they send messages via other means. They inform families that adult services exist and that transition planning will occur. Commonly, these are one-way, once-a-year notifications that may not result in true understanding. To create and maintain a parent–service provider partnership, multiple communications that occur in multiple settings over an extended period are necessary. Technology offers various means of providing information, yet not all families have access to this technology or have adopted technology as a means of getting information. Varying language needs as well as the complexity of education topics must also be a consideration as service providers develop communication practices. Two-way communication enables families and service providers to set clear goals and to identify roles and responsibilities. Effective communication includes asking families for feedback to assess the clarity of the communication. Failure to communicate effectively accounts for many conflicts in parent and school or community partnerships.

> ❝ I would like information given to all special needs parents with a clear step-by-step plan as to where they go to get services and what services to expect. ❞
>
> *A father's recommendations*

INDICATORS OF SUCCESS FOR PROACTIVE COMMUNICATION

○ Families are able to describe the transition service system and the transition services and supports available.

○ Service providers ask family members for feedback about communication efforts.

○ Families openly give their impressions and information needs.

○ Oral and written communications are understandable by all.

○ Information about transition services is provided frequently and in multiple ways such as brochures, videos, parent-student meetings, parent coffees, Web sites, listserves, wikis, Facebook, transition fairs, transition workshops, and so forth.

Be Caring and Committed

Blue-Banning and colleagues (2004) describe commitment as a key quality indicator for successful home–school partnerships. deFur et al. (2001) used the term caring as a similar construct. Families and youth respond to service providers who hold youth to appropriately high expectations, who believe that youth will achieve the goals that are set, who recognize the demands of multiply stressed families, and who encourage, listen, persist, and offer support.

Unfortunately, inherent in special education and many adult services is bureaucracy, jargon, and all too often a focus on forms, procedures, and documents. The meeting process that accompanies transition planning, where families are talked at rather than listened to, often promotes passive involvement by family members. This approach sets up an unequal power distribution, which contradicts the notion of equal participation in the process and violates the principles of a partnership described earlier. In addition, educators and adult service providers often receive training that warns against the overpersonalization of their interactions with family members as a means of maintaining objectivity; thus, meeting procedures originate from the service provider needs rather than the family context.

> ❝ I can tell you about going to back-to-school night freshman year and meeting his teacher who had no preparation in working with students with disabilities and who did not know my son's name or anything about him and did not care about whether or not his class met my son's IEP accommodations. ❞
>
> *A mother*

In reality, transition practitioners operate within a service delivery framework with standards and eligibility that often focus on deficits, as well as budgets that require consideration as transition services are negotiated. As in most professional settings, jargon exists as a means of communication between and among service providers. Specialists and agencies typically offer services tailored specifically to address student or client deficits rather than strengths. Service providers have rules, regulations, and guidelines. The system is often slow to respond to parents as it follows system policies and procedures. These system attributes often create both an atmosphere of formality and a perception that system concerns override individual outcomes and family context. In addition, these characteristics may communicate a message to families and service providers that the system alone can solve the problem.

Service providers may operate with the belief that families cannot understand the complexities of the system, which may be an erroneous assumption. Families of transition-age youth may have long histories of seeking services for their child, possibly including experience with formal complaints and due process. At the other end of the spectrum, the history may instead illustrate the withdrawal of the family from participation following years of passivity. These histories may distance the family and the service provider and challenge the demonstration of empathetic listening and reaching agreement on the joint interest of the group (deFur et al., 2001; Hanley-Maxwell et al., 1998).

INDICATORS OF SUCCESS FOR A CARING AND COMMITTED PARTNERSHIP

○ Service providers listen to family stories and cooperatively identify supports needed for the family.

○ Service providers demonstrate perseverance on behalf of youth and families.

○ Service providers demonstrate belief that the young adult with a disability can achieve his or her transition goals.

○ Service providers suspend their judgment of family status or past actions; they do not blame the family for failures.

○ Family members understand the intentions of service policy and procedures as protecting the joint interest of the transition partnership and as means to support the transition effort.

○ The service provider system uses family feedback to improve policies and procedures to be more in concert with family needs.

Give Choice and Voice

In a true partnership, each partner has both choice and voice. From a transition perspective, parents and students should be active participants in decision making and be empowered to make choices regarding transition options. Transition partners must work to ensure that all team members' voices are heard and that all have equal degree of influence on transition decisions (Blue-Banning et al., 2004). When diverse opinions exist, there is a potential for conflict. Conflict can be positive when it leads to creative solutions, but detrimental without a shared understanding of collaborative conflict resolution.

> ❝ I can tell you that when I complained, we held another IEP meeting and this was attended by special education directors and superintendents, and I was branded as a problem parent. ❞
>
> *A mother*

Transition service providers seeking to create collaborative partnerships with families must take the steps and time to fully include families and youths in the process. *Collaboration* assumes there will be parity by all participants, shared decision making, shared expertise, shared responsibility, and shared accountability. As long as service providers perceive themselves (or are perceived) as housing all the solutions, and family members are perceived as lacking valuable expertise (or as expecting unrealistic services), family and agency collaboration will be blocked. As long as all transition services remain school- or agency-based and service providers assume all responsibility, then families or youths may not recognize their own capacity, nor feel ownership of or commitment to the partnership. Service providers can help families identify their strengths and family resources that in turn will contribute to family empowerment in the transition process.

Collaborative parent and school/community service provider partnerships presume active participation by all team members, with the role of parents or youths as team leaders emerging as the transition process evolves. Ensuring that parents and youths have choices and that their voices are heard is essential to this transformation. In this partnership, service providers recognize that families and students can make different choices than what service providers might traditionally recommend. Families and students recognize that service providers may offer different suggestions. At the same time, families and students who have a voice in the process should be able to question the process without being labeled as difficult.

INDICATORS OF SUCCESS FOR GIVING CHOICE AND VOICE

- ○ Families (including the youth) are recognized for their expertise regarding the transition needs, interests, and preferences for the youth or young adult with a disability.
- ○ Transition partnerships use parent information in decision making and problem solving regarding transition services and programs.

○ Families feel safe in sharing information openly and honestly with service providers.

○ Families and service providers share responsibility for implementing and evaluating transition activities.

○ Parents or youth with disabilities share leadership roles in the transition process with service providers.

○ Team members can identify how decisions are made and how conflicts are resolved.

Problem Solve Creatively

IEP development is a team process with the intended outcome of identifying educational services that provide the student with a disability with a free appropriate education. The IEP serves as a communication tool between parent and school, and offers a unique forum for problem solving. Yet, reflecting on the parent/school conflict around IEPs, it seems as though the IEP process has lost (or never adopted) a problem-solving approach to discover the optimum ways of providing special education. Born from a civil rights framework, the IEP process has focused on policies, rules, and regulations. Unfortunately, this focus has contributed to the IEP process too often being consumed by legal documents and a focus on fear of procedural violations. The transition period for youth amplifies the need to engage in dialogue and creative problem solving; time is running out for these families and youth to benefit from the collective wisdom of professionals, parents, and students who can engage in a strategic planning process. Dialogue and creative problem solving, where all voices are heard and not judged, offers an opportunity to generate and examine possibilities not previously considered.

> ❝ There are so many options available to Emily at this time. The school transition team has been open to many possibilities for her future, and are taking her desires and wishes into consideration. They have even opened my mind about the possibility of her learning to drive. ❞
>
> *A mother, discussing the collaborative efforts of her daughter's transition team*

Person-centered planning processes such as Making Action Plans (MAPS; Forest & Lusthaus, 1990) or Planning Alternative Tomorrows with Hope, (PATH; Pearpoint, O'Brien, & Forest, 1993) offer a way to look at the student holistically and generate creative actions to take on behalf of youth and their families. Appreciative Inquiry (Cooperrider, Whitney, & Stavros, 2008) is another methodology that visualizes the future, focuses on relationships, and may prove helpful as service providers facilitate transition planning.

Allotted meeting time may challenge the use of these methodologies at every transition planning event, yet the principles of these processes can be implemented in every IEP meeting. Staying future focused, listening to stories that describe experiences, and brainstorming possibilities without evaluation are approaches that will generate creativity. Transition planning teams may avoid creative problem solving because sometimes people fret that an idea, once stated, becomes a plan rather than point of beginning.

To creatively problem solve, families and service providers must be open to new ideas and possibilities. Individuals must be risk takers and action takers to creatively plan and deliver transition services to youths with disabilities.

In his book *The 7 Habits of Highly Effective People,* Stephen Covey (1989) outlined the difference between being reactive versus proactive. Consider a transition team's attempts to develop transition services when there seem to be few resources available. A reactive response would be, "There's nothing I can do; we have such few resources." A proactive response would be "Let's look at the alternatives that are available." When agency policies and procedures seem to be a barrier, some people reactively tend to say, "They won't let me do that, because this is the policy of the school or agency." A proactive alternative is, "Let's think about how the policy can be used to support the transition activities being suggested." While brainstorming service alternatives, people reactively might say, "If only we could realistically do this." A proactive response would be, "I wonder if we could do some part of this activity or something similar." Covey suggests that individuals take a day and evaluate the language around them for reactivity versus proactivity. Listen for reactive phrases such as "I can't," "They make me so mad," or "Yes, but." At the same time, listen for proactive language such as "I choose," "I will," or "I can." Practitioners should evaluate their own language to see if it fosters creative problem solving.

INDICATORS OF SUCCESS FOR CREATIVE PROBLEM SOLVING

○ Service providers and families brainstorm and evaluate options that differ from the traditional services usually offered in the transition process.

○ IEP transition meetings focus on options and problem solving rather than procedure.

○ Service providers, families, and youths are willing to take risks and try new ideas.

○ Service providers and families use proactive language and focus on solutions.

○ Service providers have a toolbox to use for facilitation, strategic planning, and problem solving.

Make Connections

Partners share responsibilities; they engage in activities toward a common goal. They reinforce one another and support one another. They are equal. Family members can demonstrate these mutual support characteristics in the transition partnership more readily when families have the needed connections.

> ❝ Who do I ask questions of? Who is that person? Just let me know whose door I should be knocking on to get these services and who to go to if they need to be improved. ❞
>
> *A parent who had expressed concerns that she did not*
> *know who could offer transition help*

INDICATORS OF SUCCESS FOR EFFECTIVE CONNECTIONS

○ School-based service providers introduce families to adult service providers specific to their children's potential support needs.

○ Practitioners identify social support networks within the immediate community (e.g., local advocacy groups, support groups, and other parents who have had similar transition experiences).

○ Practitioners offer structured opportunities (transition fairs, transition workshops, etc.) for families to meet community transition resources and disseminate written materials describing community transition options and supports.

○ Youth with disabilities serve as coaches or mentors to other youth and young adults with disabilities. Families offer to serve as coaches or mentors to other families in the transition process.

○ Family members, including youth and young adults with disabilities, serve on interagency boards, transition planning groups, school committees, and so forth.

○ States or districts establish a set of family connections indicators that are used to evaluate the support for family involvement in the transition process.

Take Action

New patterns of behaviors by individuals and by agencies must occur to embrace a collaborative partnership approach for transition planning and services. Sometimes, the process or the problem seems too big and the solutions too abstract. It is possible to spend excessive time analyzing and assessing a problem, trying to find a perfect solution—and no time acting. Parents would prefer that service providers proceed and take a step at a time, where experience and reflection foster solutions, than to engage in all talk and no action.

> " Stop exploring . . . do! "
>
> *A parent offering advice on transition services*

Blue-Banning et al. (2004) remind us that team members must believe that others on the team are competent. From a parent perspective, this means that service providers acted on behalf of the student and implemented effective transition services. Families want to see transition plans being implemented, not just discussed. Where one begins, or how one begins, may not be as important as that one begins.

> " By asking questions and being an active participant in my child's IEP process, I was able to achieve my goal of making educated decisions for my child while also making positive contributions towards my child's future success—that felt so good! "
>
> *A parent*

Accountability and progress monitoring are critical to achieving successful transition outcomes. Parents, students, and service providers need to create a transition activities annual work plan, with a system of reporting and review that can manage and track the implementation of the planned transition activities for each year. Teams can extend the process of the progress monitoring required for IEP goals to the implementation of transition activities, creating a case management plan that ensures transition activities are completed. Action plans detail roles, responsibilities, and timelines for professionals, families, and youth. All participants have an active role in the implementation of transition activities; monitoring the action plan demonstrates a commitment to put the plan into action and to evaluate the impact of the transition activities.

INDICATORS OF SUCCESS FOR TAKING ACTION

○ The transition team develops, monitors, and evaluates action plans with clear roles, responsibilities, and timelines.

○ Professionals, parents, and students have roles and responsibilities in the implementation of transition activities.

○ Parents, students, and service providers share ownership in the outcome of activities.

○ Actions that do not work are viewed as learning opportunities, not failures, and new strategies are developed.

Reflect and Celebrate

Effective transition planning requires that families and service providers adopt a strengths-based paradigm rather than the traditional deficit paradigm of disability and special education. The stigma of special education and focus on weaknesses does little to promote positive outcomes for youth or young adults. Strengths represent the avenues through which we learn and grow; abilities and skills shape our careers, our recreation, and our relationships. Promoting the abilities of youth with disabilities as they transition from school to postschool life supports this strengths-based approach.

Collaborative partnerships take time to celebrate transition accomplishments, both small and large. Education and community service providers spend a great deal of energy on process and procedure, often to the exclusion of congratulating themselves or families or youths. Success builds both competence and confidence, essential skills for ongoing posttransition work. Celebrating the work of the group and of the committed individuals involved provides ongoing encouragement and time for reflection.

INDICATORS OF SUCCESS FOR REFLECTIONS AND CELEBRATIONS

○ Service providers focus on the abilities of youth and young adults with disabilities.

○ Families receive regular communication from practitioners acknowledging small as well as large accomplishments toward transition goals.

○ Transition partnerships publicly recognize the successes and accomplishments of youth with disabilities in the transition process.

○ Service providers and families credit the partnership for transition successes.

Conclusion

Mutual trust and respect represent the foundation of collaborative partnerships. Yet, trust only develops when we can predict positive behavior from our partners, and when we are confident that we can depend on one another. Trust seldom exists after a first meeting, but builds upon history . Prior history with service providers will be the lens through which families view initial attempts at creating a partnership. Likewise, service providers' histories with prior students, clients, and their families influence their expectations and attitudes. These histories, plus the openness with which people share their experiences and expectations, will determine how long it takes to create an environment that allows trust and respect to develop. Collaborative partnerships are not likely to result from a single transition planning meeting or a single event. Trusting partnerships require cumulative efforts and actions over time, where service providers and family members consistently demonstrate collaborative transition partnership behaviors. They have to actually practice being partners. Service providers must take the leadership role in this practice. Because practice makes permanent, practice should be based on a strategic foundation. Practice that engages in the 10 actions of the Family Partnership Model presented in Figure 1 can build collaborative partnerships with families.

The Family Partnership Model can also serve as diagnostic tool when there are challenges in the family/service provider relationship. Team members can reflect on these questions: Have we made the process student- and family-centered, in an environment of cultural responsiveness? Is the commitment to the student and his future evident? Do we have a shared vision for this student's future? What means of communication have we used to build capacity of families and service providers to understand the transition process and options? Has the process offered choice and voice in our collaborative efforts and problem solving? Have we acted on our agreements and reflected on accomplishments? Service providers who adopt a partnership philosophy, acting consistently in accordance with partnership principles, set the stage for families to join the collaborative transition partnership.

REFERENCES

Alliance for Excellent Education. (2007). *In need of improvement: NCLB and high schools.* Washington, DC: Author.

Arndt, S. A., Konrad, M., & Test, D. W. (2006). Effects of self-directed IEP on student participation in planning meetings. *Remedial and Special Education, 27,* 194–207.

Blue-Banning, M., Summers, J. A., Frankland, H. C., Nelson, L., & Beegle, G. (2004). Dimensions of family and professional partnerships: Constructive guidelines for collaboration. *Exceptional Children, 70,* 167–184.

Collet-Klingenberg, L. (1998). The reality of best practices in transition: A case study. *Exceptional Children, 65,* 67–72.

Cooperrider, D., Whitney, D., & Stavros, J. (2008). *The appreciative inquiry handbook for leaders of change.* San Francisco: Berrett-Koehler.

Covey, S. (1989). *The seven habits of highly effective people.* New York: Simon and Schuster.

deFur, S. (2003). Parents as collaborators: Building collaborative partnerships with school-based and-community-based providers. In D. Wandry & A. Pleet (Eds.), *A practitioner's guide to involving families in secondary transition.* Arlington, VA: Council for Exceptional Children.

deFur, S., Todd-Allen, M., & Getzel, E. (2001). Parent participation in the transition planning process. *Career Development for Exceptional Individuals, 24,* 19–36.

Eptein, J. L. (2005). School-initiated family and community partnerships. In T. Erb (Ed.), *This we believe in action: Implementing successful middle level schools* (pp. 77–96). Westerville, OH: National Middle School Association.

Family Strengthening Policy Center. (2004, October). *Parental involvement in education* (Policy Brief No. 3). Washington, DC: National Human Services Assembly. Retrieved October 1, 2008, from http://www.nassembly.org/fspc/practice/documents/ ParentalInvolvementBrief2.pdf

Forest, M., & Lusthaus, E. (1990). Everyone belongs with MAPS action planning system. *TEACHING Exceptional Children, 22*(2), 32–35.

Gil-Kashiabara, E., Hogansen, J. M., Geenen, S., Powers, K., & Powers, L. E. (2007). Improving transition outcomes for marginalized youth. *Career Development for Exceptional Individuals, 30,* 80–91.

Hammer, M. R. (2004). Using the self-advocacy strategy to increase student participation in IEP conferences. *Intervention in School and Clinic, 39,* 295–300.

Hanley-Maxwell, C., Pogoloff, S. M., & Whitney-Thomas, J. (1998). Families—The heart of transition. In F. Rusch & J. Chadsey (Eds.), *Beyond high school: Transition from school to work* (pp. 234–264). Belmond, CA: Wadsworth.

Harry, B. (2008). Collaboration with culturally and linguistically diverse families: Ideal versus reality. *Exceptional Children, 72,* 372–388.

Harry, B., Allen, N., & McLaughlin, M. (1995). Communication versus compliance: African-American parents' involvement in special education. *Exceptional Children, 61,* 364–377.

Harvard Family Research Project. (2007). *Family involvement in middle and high school students' education.* Cambridge, MA: Harvard Graduate School of Education, Author.

Hasazi, S., Furney, K., & Destefano, L. (1999). Implementing the IDEA transition mandates. *Exceptional Children, 65,* 555–566.

Hodgkinson, H. (2000). *Secondary schools in the new millennium: Demographic certainties, social realities.* Reston, VA: National Association of Secondary School Principals.

Individuals With Disabilities Education Improvement Act of 2004, 20 U.S.C. § 1400 *et seq.* (2004).

Knight, J. (2002). *Partnership learning fieldbook.* Lawrence, KS: The University of Kansas Center for Research on Learning.

Lindstrom, L., Doren, B., Metheny, J., Johnson, P., & Zane, C. (2007). Transition to employment: Role of the family in career development. *Exceptional Children, 73,* 348–366.

Martin, J., Marshall, L., & Sale, P. (2004). A 3-year study of middle, junior, high, and high school IEP meetings. *Exceptional Children , 70,* 285–297.

McGahee-Kovac, M. (2002). *A student's guide to the IEP.* Retrieved October 30, 2008, from www.ldonline.org/article/5944

No Child Left Behind Act of 2001, 20 U.S.C. § 6301 *et seq.* (2002).

Pearpoint, J., O'Brien, J., & Forest, M. (1993). *PATH: A workbook for planning positive possible futures and planning alternative tomorrows with hope for schools, organizations, businesses, and families* (2nd ed.). Toronto: Inclusion Press.

Powers, L., Turner, A., Matuszewski, J., Wilson, R., & Loesch, C. (1999). A qualitative analysis of student involvement in transition planning. *The Journal for Vocational Special Needs Education, 21*(3), 18–26.

Schwartz, A., Jacobson, J., & Holburn, S. (2000). Defining person centeredness: Results of two consensus methods. *Education and Training in Mental Retardation and Developmental Disabilities, 35,* 235–249.

Storms, J., O'Leary, E., & Williams, J. (2000). *The Individuals with Disabilities Education Act of 1997 transition requirements: A guide for states, districts, schools, universities and families.* Minneapolis: University of Minnesota College of Education & Human Development and U.S. Department of Education Office of Special Education Programs.

Thoma, C., Rogan, P., & Baker, S. (2001). Student involvement in transition planning: Unheard voices. *Education and Training in Mental Retardation and Developmental Disabilities, 36,* 16–29.

U.S. Census Bureau. (2000). *Overview of race and Hispanic origin.* Retrieved February, 23, 2009, from http://www.census.gov/population/www/socdemo/race.html

Wagner, M., Newman, L., Cameto, R., Levine, P., & Marder, C. (2007). *Perceptions and expectations of youth with disabilities: A special topic report of findings from the National Longitudinal Transition Study-2* (NLTS2; NCSER 2007-3006). Menlo Park, CA: SRI International.

Wehmeyer, M., Morningstar, M., & Husted, D. (1999). *Family involvement in transition planning and program implementation.* Austin: Pro-Ed.

Wood, R. M., Rogers, R., & Yancey, G. (2006). Academic enrichment for students and ESL classes for parents strengthen a community-based middle school. *Middle School Journal, 38,* 44-50.

Zhang, D., & Stecker, P. (2001). Student involvement in transition planning: Are we there yet? *Education and Training in Mental Retardation and Developmental Disabilities, 36,* 293–303.

ABOUT THE AUTHOR

SHARON DEFUR, a Professor of Special Education at the College of William and Mary, conducts program evaluation and research in the area of secondary education and transition of youth and young adults with disabilities. Her specific interests include student and family-centered strategic transition planning, teacher preparation, and secondary curriculum effects on transition outcomes. Dr. deFur's career in special education includes public school teaching as well as serving as the coordinator of transition services for the Commonwealth of Virginia. Dr. deFur is a former President of the Council for Exceptional Children's Division on Career Development and Transition.

4

Parents as Instructors in Their Youths' Emergent Independence

Michael J. Ward

ESSENTIAL QUESTIONS

○ What are the opportunities and challenges for parents as instructors as they foster self-determination in their children during the transition process?

○ What are the underlying values and beliefs that practitioners need to validate to establish a shared investment in emergent independence?

○ What are prerequisite skills and knowledge parents and practitioners need to energize this parental role?

The home is one of several spheres that simultaneously influence a child's development and acquisition of learning (Carter, 2003). Parents often serve as a child's strongest advocates as well as "teach, model and guide their children" (Rockwell, Andrew, & Hawley, 1996). Because the parent is the central contributor to a child's education, schools that are committed to drawing on the resources of all stakeholders recognize the potential of the parent to be a partner in instructional planning and delivery. Aside from children's parents or guardians, classroom teachers are the "most significant adults" in children's lives. "When teachers strive to work collaboratively with their students' families in honoring and including students, results are astonishing" (O'Shea, O'Shea, Algozzine, & Hammitte, 2001, p. 11).

For school personnel to establish and facilitate collaboration with parents, they need to build trust with parents that they are not there to usurp the parental role nor pretend that they have expert knowledge on developing the child's skills in every domain; they are there to work collaboratively for the benefit of the child. As Wolfendale (2002) conceptualized, the parent–professional partnership recognizes reciprocal expertise. Parents are

53

experts on their own children, but most need information, advice, and support in fulfilling this role as instructional partners, as well as using that instruction to foster self-determination skills in their children.

Benefits of Parents as Instructors

Successful parent involvement nurtures their relationship and partnership with the school and other service providers. It strengthens bonds between home and school, parent and practitioner, and school and community (Carter, 2003). Collaboration facilitates the child's goals being mutually developed and implemented by the parents and practitioners. Schools that involve parents recognize the important connection between "what is taught [at school] and what is encouraged, practiced, discussed and celebrated at home" (Epstein, 2001, p. 510). More specifically, parents can help reinforce the school's efforts by supporting, encouraging, and motivating their children; monitoring their work; celebrating their progress; and engaging in interactions that help children complete homework and do well in school (Epstein; Hoover-Dempsey & Sandler, 1995).

Students whose parents are involved in their education show higher academic achievement (Henderson & Mapp, 2002; Patrikakou, 2004), improved attendance, higher aspirations for postsecondary education and career development (Caplan, Hall, Lubin, & Fleming, 1997), and improved social competence (Webster-Stratton, Reid, & Hammond, 2001). Parent involvement pays off in improved student achievement, improved school effectiveness, and increased parent and community satisfaction (San Diego City Schools, 1991).

The home offers children their earliest opportunities to express choices, solve problems and make decisions, experience control, and exhibit competence in a wide range of activities, typically by watching the actions of their parents and other adults (Cook, Brotherson, Weigel-Garrey, & Mize, 1996; Wehmeyer, Morningstar, & Husted, 1999). Home settings present realistic opportunities to generalize and reinforce skills learned in school. Childhood choices start with opportunities to make decisions in the home about when, where, and how to perform activities of daily living, such as eating, dressing, self-care, and play.

Parents have primary responsibility for teaching their children many life-coping skills. They teach their children to dress, feed, and care for themselves, navigate safely around their neighborhood, and complete their homework so they can progress academically. Ultimately, as children become adolescents, the parents' instructional role should move toward facilitating their youth's independence and self-determination; the role of parents as instructor of core skills extends into the realm of teaching skills for owning and managing one's adult responsibilities.

Supporting Parents in the Transfer of Ownership and Advocacy to the Adolescent

One of the most challenging tasks for transition practitioners is to help parents see their sons and daughters with disabilities as capable of managing their own lives to the maximum extent possible with an appropriate level of support. Decision making is a natural step in the maturation process and is strongly encouraged by the Individuals With Disabilities Improvement Act of 2004 (IDEA), which requires the transfer of decision making and advocacy rights from parents to young persons upon reaching the age of majority. Not only do adolescents need support and guidance from their parents in their initial attempts in these areas, but parents may need help from transition practitioners in how to best pass on these responsibilities.

Students with disabilities need support from both practitioners and parents in developing skills for independence, through the teaching of self-determination skills. Halloran (1993) described self-determination as the

> ultimate goal of education . . . . [The acquisition of self-determination] should not be assumed to be a natural occurrence but rather the result of purposeful strategies, properly implemented, to achieve the desired outcome of independence . . . . Actualizing this emphasis would require a major change in the current approach to educating, parenting, or planning for children and youth with disabilities. (p. 214)

Field, Hoffman, and Posch (1997) believe that self-determination begins with knowing and valuing oneself. This means that young people accept themselves for who they are, including their abilities and also their limitations. Adolescents get a sense of this from those around them, including family members and teachers, so it is critical that these significant others provide a consistent message that they are capable, competent individuals who have a claim to community participation with support as necessary. Because adolescence is a time of striving to perform activities by themselves, and asking for help can be seen as a behavior contrary to this developmental phase, it is critical that parents, teachers, and peers reinforce that it is acceptable for the adolescent to request help. When relationships are built on mutual interests, respect, and trust, helping and supporting others becomes a natural part of these interactions.

Because the goal of education is to support adult independence, it is essential that parents reinforce and implement self-determination skills within the context of activities performed in the home setting (Zhang, Katsiyannis, & Zhang, 2002). However, families need training and information on effective practices to develop the skills to promote this concept at home beginning with early education (Zhang, Wehmeyer, & Chen, 2005). In a study of parent and teacher views toward self-determination, parents of secondary students with disabilities recognized the importance of teaching this concept at school (Grigal, Neubert, Moon, & Graham, 2003). Collaborative efforts between parents and teachers are more likely to be successful in promoting self-determination than by teacher instruction alone (Lee, Palmer, Turnbull, & Wehmeyer, 2006).

Since the Office of Special Education Programs funded the original 26 model demonstration projects on self-determination in the early 1990s (Ward, 1996), there has been general recognition in the field of the importance of self-determination and its need to be addressed systematically through a specific curriculum. It is imperative that youth with disabilities receive sustained training and practice in both school and home to develop skills necessary for self-determination, and that they have multiple opportunities to practice these skills (Field, Martin, Miller, Ward, & Wehmeyer, 1998; Ward & Kohler, 1996). Self-determination skill training needs to begin with very young children across home and school environments in order to prevent the cycle of dependency, learned helplessness, and feelings of inability (Doll, Sands, Wehmeyer, & Palmer, 1996).

> ❝ My parents played a significant role in molding my self-advocacy skills. When I was young, I lacked verbal skills so my parents searched for books that would show pictures about feelings. They always wanted to know how I felt at times and encouraged me to describe my feelings. They would often say, "Use words, Chris." I became expressive and learned to make it clear whenever I did not understand what was going on. It is my parents I have to thank, for teaching me to become the assertive and social person I am today. Throughout my educational career dating back to elementary school, I have always had to be assertive and expressive of my needs towards my teachers and fellow classmates due to my hearing impairment. Some of those needs included using FM transmitter (an amplifier) with the teacher, sitting up in the front row of my class, taking extra time in tests, and receiving classroom tutoring. In each of my classes, I always wanted to learn and so if I happened to not hear something that was said, I would ask questions either during class or after class. Looking back, I am very thankful for the invaluable role that my parents played in my life. ❞
>
> *Chris Gerbetz, Student, The Ohio State University*

Challenges in Supporting Parents

Although most parents view learning good decision making as a process all young people should accomplish in becoming independent adults, they may be more hesitant in allowing their young person with a disability to be involved in this process. Four reasons for this hesitancy might be considered:

Overprotection, the belief that their young person is vulnerable to getting hurt or will make a dangerous decision that would jeopardize his or her safety, can be taken to the extreme. Consider the recent phenomenon of "helicopter parents." This label refers to oppressive parents who tend to hover over their teenage and adults children, keeping in constant contact and often meddling in their personal and professional relationships (Damast, 2007). They tend to micromanage every aspect of their children's lives, including schoolwork. Such behavior can damage emotional and academic growth and inhibit adolescents from learning to solve their own problems and conflicts (Cleaver, 2008).

Fear of their young person's failure coupled with belief that having a disability is enough trauma without experiencing the distress of making bad decisions may inhibit parents. Parents may have difficulty understanding that risk, failure, and adversity can be beneficial in helping most adolescents test the limits of what they can and cannot achieve. Perske (1972) called for the opportunity for all people with disabilities to experience the "dignity of risk":

> The world in which we live is not always safe, secure and pre-dictable . . . . Every day that we wake up and live in the hours of that day, there is a possibility of being thrown up against a situa-tion where we may have to risk everything, even our lives. This is the way the real world is. We must work to develop every human resource within us in order to prepare for these days. To deny any person their fair share of risk experiences is to further cripple them for healthy living. (p. 199)

An attitude of *pragmatic ease* leads the adult to simply do the task rather than going through the extra time and effort to teach the youth to do it, but placing adolescents with disabilities in a perpetual state of childhood can stifle the development of self-determination. Sooner or later, parents need to be reminded that these youths need to learn to do their own laundry, select their own clothes, clean up their own messes, make their own trans-portation arrangements, and take charge of personal hygiene. Research indicates that parents of children with disabilities are less likely to involve them in performing household chores, making their own decisions, setting goals and recognizing their needs, engaging in trial-and-error activities, or in making choices and decisions (Zhang, 2005).

An *authoritarian parenting style,* in which parents expect children to comply with established rules and household regimens, often interprets self-determined behavior as rebellion. These parents, perhaps because of their long held and oftentimes unquestioned cultural values, believe that adolescents and young adults should demonstrate respect for their elders by adhering to their wishes. Yet a natural part of developmental matura-tion, according to adolescent theory, includes breaking away from the nuclear family structure and activating abilities to make independent deci-sions and increase autonomous behaviors (Kochhar-Bryant & Greene, 2009).

Strategies for Fostering Self-Determination in Daily Living Activities

Practitioners can support parents in their efforts to promote self-determina-tion by beginning with simple steps. Parents should encourage their sons and daughters to practice making decisions at an early age by providing as much information as they need to make good decisions. Such decisions can focus on what to wear and helping to plan the family's dinner menu. Most adolescents will learn quickly that bad decisions lead to negative conse-quences and, through parental support and guidance, will become more comfortable making more responsible decisions (Guskey & Andermanm 2008). As they become more confident in making decisions, adolescents can begin to make larger decisions that will affect their lives, without being afraid of taking such risks.

The Self-Determined Learning Model of Support

A seminal student–parent–teacher self-determination instructional strategy is the self-determined learning model of support (SDLMS), which has three phases: setting a goal, developing and implementing an action plan to achieve the goal, and modifying the goal or plan in relation to evaluated progress (Agran, Wehmeyer, Cavin, & Palmer, 2008; Lee et al., 2006). The goal of this strategy is to teach students a process that facilitates their movement from a state of not having their needs and interests satisfied to one where they are satisfied.

This strategy gives parents a tool for supporting and encouraging their young adult's self-determination in the acquisition and implementation of, and the accountability for, skills in a range of domains such as daily living activities, interpersonal relationships, postsecondary education, and employment. The strategy leads the young person through a series of steps to learn most skill sets: (a) identify the skill set within a specific domain; (b) identify the range of potential instructional methods; (c) choose the most appropriate method that responds to any individual's unique learning styles; (d) implement instruction; (e) reinforce success; and (f) evaluate progress, including teaching students how to self-regulate, and make changes if necessary. Each step requires objectivity and that the parent and their young adult collect as much information as possible. Teachers and other practitioners can help parents design and implement a strategy to assist in teaching a specific skill, as well as provide expert information about possible alternatives to any potential challenges to teaching that skill.

The Self-Determination Instructional Partnership

In deference to Wehmeyer and his colleagues who developed SDLMS (Wehmeyer, Palmer, Agran, Mithaug, & Martin, 2000), for the model to truly be an instructional approach that supports the student's self-determination, the student must be actively involved and to some extent in control of every phase of the learning process. Depending on the specific disability, students may need assistance in selecting and implementing these activities. This assistance should be the result of a partnership with parents and teachers where advice and mentoring is offered to support the maximum degree of students' self-determination yet also ensure their safety: the self-determination instructional partnership (SDIP).

Identify necessary skills. The first step in developing the SDIP is to determine the skill(s) to be taught. Teachers, parents, and students have their lists of skills each feels is most important. The key is to identify priorities and develop a consensus list of skills to be learned, recognizing that they are all important but allowing sufficient flexibility to meet everyone's needs. This process is particularly meaningful to maintain the student's continued ownership of the process. Tomlison (2008) refers to this match between priorities and needs as *fit* and requires that what students are asked to learn relates to what they care about. Students are more likely to learn skills that allow them to do things they want to do and that help them make sense of their world.

Determine methodology. After identifying the specific skill to be learned, the next step is to determine the most appropriate instructional method for teaching this skill. Regardless of the method, it should provide both information to increase the young person's skill knowledge and opportunities to practice these newly learned skills (Ward & Kohler, 1996; Wehmeyer, 1999). Students with disabilities have individual learning styles, and transition teachers are aware of which style works best. Although parents have used a range of approaches to teach their adolescent important skills, they may not be aware of their adolescent's individual learning style and even less aware of the best approach to maximize that style. As part of the transition process to postsecondary education and employment, students need know how they best assimilate information and be able to convey this to their supervisors and professors. Therefore, it is important for teachers to discuss with parents and youth learning styles and offer coaching on the various instructional approaches to maximize them. Working with their parents to identify the most appropriate instructional method to learn new transition skills helps students become aware of how they learn best. Practitioners need to not only help parents understand these methods and strategies so they can use them to develop their children's skills, but also to transfer ownership of the skill use to their increasingly independent and self-determined youth. This does not mean drafting parents into becoming pedagogical experts, but rather supporting them as they reinforce needed skills in their children while fostering their growing independence. Ideally, the young person should be involved in this process, through practicing the specified skill and also providing ongoing feedback about the instructional approach (e.g., "It's hard for me to follow the steps when you only say them. Show me the steps while you say them, and I think I'll learn better.").

There are primarily five methods that parents can use for teaching foundational skills to their children that lead to independent use, application, and finally self-determined venues:

1. *Direct instruction* is the method most like what a teacher might use in a classroom, and sometimes it is appropriate for a parent to use it at home or in the community. In this method a parent and child agree to focus some time to directly teach a skill, such as how to prepare a certain recipe, how to sort laundry and use the washing machine, or how to balance a checkbook. One cannot engage in choosing a particular course of action unless the skills needed to perform that course of action are intact. Often youth will need reinforcement using other methods, but the direct instruction method is an efficient first step.

2. *Problem solving* is a method for teaching self-determination skills that youth will be able to use repeatedly to take charge of situations. According to Vaughn, Bos, and Schumm (1997), the goal is "to teach students to identify their problems, goals, and a wide range of alternative strategies for effectively solving their problems" (p. 85). They describe four components critical to the process of problem solving: (a) problem identification, (b) generating alternative solutions, (c) identifying and evaluating the consequences of the alternative solutions, and (d) implementing a solution. A critical ingredient of this strategy is that students must feel acceptance and trust that the person teaching them

to work through the problem cares about them, no matter how difficult the problem or frustrating the behavior. A problem-solving conference is built on a foundation of positive rapport, established by acknowledging the adolescent's feelings and encouragement by the parent or teacher, and will not be effective if it is laden with blame or anger (Crowe, 2008). By having students in the center of problem solving, they are taught not only to solve the current problem, but also to be self-reflective and to learn a process for solving future problems.

3. The *modeling method* often occurs outside the awareness of both the parent and the youth. The daughter watches how her mother talks to the sales clerk when returning an item. The son notices how his father responds when mother asks him to replace a light bulb. Children have unconsciously observed and imitated parents' modeled behavior from the earliest ages, beginning with learning to talk and walk. The procedure of modeling involves observing another individual (a model) perform that behavior (Elliott & Gresham, 1991). Modeling especially exposes children to competent models of social skills so that they can imitate or reproduce the observed behavior. In classrooms, modeling can be made most effective by (a) setting the stage for what is to be modeled by introducing the behavior to be modeled, (b) specifying the behavior to be modeled, (c) providing feedback to children on how well they imitated the behavior, (d) providing opportunities for practice, and (e) rewarding correct reproductions and generalization of the behavior. Parents would not use such a formalized approach, but it is helpful for them to be aware of the various components. Once parents and youth are aware of this method, they can consciously use it to teach and learn a new skill.

4. Through *taking advantage of "teachable moments"* parents can turn a negative situation into a learning experience (Johns, Crowley, & Guetzloe, 2005). Often when the youth is "stuck" and doesn't know how to proceed, it's the perfect opportunity to teach the youth a skill. There are teachable moments everywhere in life if one knows how to recognize them. Adolescents can be taught how to clean up after themselves when they have just dropped a pot of spaghetti; how to respond appropriately when introduced to a neighbor in the mall; how to handle frustration when their computer freezes up; how to call the doctor to schedule an appointment for a sports physical. Practitioners and parents should also use this event to teach the students what he could do if this situation occurs again.

5. *Coaching* is a method that works well in combination with other methods to reinforce ongoing practice, adoption, and appropriately selective application of a new skill. Verbal coaching depends primarily upon the child's understanding of language and verbal concepts (Elliott & Gresham, 1991; Gresham, 1982) and includes three components: (a) presentating expectations for behavior, (b) opportunities for practice, and (c) response feedback and discussion (Gresham, 1998). However, coaching doesn't have to be primarily verbal. A coach, whether on the football field, in the music studio, or at home, is someone who believes in and respects the learner's ability to learn, apply, and eventually select the

skill as an appropriate option. The coach listens without judgment; honors confidentiality; uses guiding questions or other forms of prompting so that the learner can reflect on his own practice; elicits solutions and strategies from the person being coached; gathers data to set goals, analyze issues, and measure success; and communicates effectively to promote thinking and learning (Carr, Herman, & Harris, 2005, p. 82). Coaching is becoming the preferred method of learning for adults because it empowers the individual to take the lead in engaging in lifelong learning and personal improvement.

Self-regulation and evaluation. Finally, when attempting to build and maintain any new skills, be it life, academic or social, positive feedback is essential (Sulzer-Azaroff & Mayer, 1991; Wolery & Lane, 2005). To maintain and generalize the skills beyond the "training" setting, it is important to provide students with reinforcement of the skill in other settings, which can be faded out over time so that the targeted skills will be incorporated into the student's repertoire and generalize to other settings, other people, and over time.

The ultimate goal of all skill instruction is for adolescents to assume responsibility not only for judging the effectiveness of their own decisions, but also regulating their own learning. To do this, they need to be central in the process of setting goals, determining appropriate plans to reach those goals, and adjusting actions to complete plans. Self-regulation requires them to evaluate their progress by monitoring and tracking performance outcomes, then comparing their results with goals and performance expectations they set when they first identified the skills selected to be learned (Wehmeyer, 1999). Self-monitoring occurs when adolescents can observe whether they have performed the identified skill to the established criteria. A final step in this process teaches adolescents self-reinforcement where they commend themselves for a job well done (Wehmeyer, Hughes, Agran, Garner, & Yeager, 2003). This can be accomplished through positive self-talk ("I feel good that I learned how to use the bus to go downtown.") and self-reinforcement ("I successfully made it downtown, so I will reward myself and buy some ice cream.").

Applying the Self-Determination Instructional Partnership to Various Domains

Daily Living Skills

Daily living skills can range from feeding and dressing to getting around one's community and shopping for food in a grocery store. It is hoped that young people with disabilities are as independent as possible in performing many activities of daily living by the time they reach adolescence, and many will be. However, if some skills have not been mastered, parents should be encouraged to take a look again at teaching these skills in preparation for their youth's transition to adult life. This is especially critical because at this point, the goal is to move youth beyond directed use in the home to appropriately selective use in other environments. Perhaps parents were reluctant to teach these skills in the past because of the extra time that it took the child to do it, they never got around to buying the necessary but expensive adaptive equipment, or it was just easier for mom or dad to perform the task. Parents may be reluctant to admit that they won't always be around to help and as both parents and child get older, it may be more difficult for parents to maneuver a bigger, heavier child with significant disabilities or change a habitual dependent behavior. However, such realities may be difficult for parents to proactively accept without support (and, often, gentle confrontation) by outside parties. Special education practitioners (teachers, aides, occupational and physical therapists) can offer parents and students alternative instructional techniques to develop the targeted skill along with information on any helpful adaptive equipment or home modification if needed.

66 When I went to college, it was before the passage of Section 504 and the ADA, and it wasn't exactly accessible. Vocational Rehabilitation was giving my roommate, Emmett, a stipend to help me with some activities of daily living. The shower in the common bathroom had a step up so he had to help me sit on the floor of the shower and then come back in about 10 minutes to get me back into my wheelchair. He would invariably get to talking to someone (or fall asleep) and forget to come back. Time would go by, and sometimes someone would come into the bathroom, and I could tell him to get Emmett. However, sometimes no one would come by for a long time, and I would turn into a prune! I decided to look for other alternatives and found that each floor had a private suite that the college turned into a study room, which wasn't used that often. While again its bathroom wasn't accessible, there were enough handholds that I could get in and out of the shower by myself. I believe in the old adage that necessity (avoiding looking shriveled) is the mother of invention . . . and self-determination. 99

Michael Ward

For adolescents, it may be time to break old habits and practice new behaviors. Self-determination is part of the maturation process and includes the use of independent daily living skills outside the home where help from parents may not always available. How does the young person in a wheelchair spend hours at the mall with peers without assistance or independence in using the bathroom? How can they make purchases without mastering money skills? Can the young college student handle his own laundry? Will the young adult be able to identify a needed accommodation and ask for it appropriately? When is not having the skill more awkward than asking for help? However, asking for help is a skill in itself and young people with disabilities must feel comfortable enough with themselves and with friends or others in the setting to ask for it.

Increased independence in traveling around the community is one example of the activities of daily living that should be taught and learned. Transportation is important because transition practitioners report that it is a major barrier to successful transition. If young adults, with or without practitioner assistance, find jobs in their communities, but have no viable means of getting to the place of employment, their efforts are for naught. Therefore, it is extremely important that transition practitioners, in tandem with the family and the young adult, identify or develop transportation options appropriate to the young adult's needs. Transportation options could include using the public transportation system, car pooling with friends and family members, or obtaining a driver's license. The last option is associated with the most risk, and is, therefore, the one that parents may be reluctant to pursue. Transition practitioners and parents should help young adults look at all transportation options so the young adult can make an informed choice about which one or combination of options would work best.

SCENARIO 1: BEN. Ben has made plans with friends to stay at school for a basketball game after the school bus leaves and wants his mother to pick him up at 4:30. Unfortunately, his younger brother, Joe, has a dentist appointment and his mom won't be able to pick Ben up until much later. They both view the problem differently: Ben sees the problem as Mom being inflexible; Mom sees it as Ben being irresponsible and selfish for waiting until the last minute to make plans and expecting her to help support them. Neither has correctly identified the actual problem: finding a way to safely get Ben home after the game. The first step in finding a real solution is to take emotions out of the problem and focus on the real issue, identifying needed skills or information. Does Ben need to acquire skills for planning in advance, or skills in identifying and selecting transportation options? How will he learn these skills? Ben and his mom decide he needs to learn to problem solve, and master the process: identify the problem, generate alternative solutions, identify and evaluate the consequences of the alternative solutions, and implement a solution. Identifying all possible solutions may take some creativity and brainstorming; no possible alternatives should initially be discounted. Can Ben ask a friend's parent to bring him home? Can Ben use public transportation, and is it available between school and home? Can he wait at the school until Mom gets him about 6 o'clock? Can he contact Dad to pick him up earlier? Can the school offer assistance—and does Ben have the skills to ask for it?

Problem solving as an approach necessitates evaluating options; in this case, Ben and his mom have to consider and discuss barriers and strategies for each potential solution, and formulate alternatives if initial options are not viable. Ben determines the following: the parents of his friends who live nearby don't have cars big enough for his wheelchair; not every bus on the two routes he needs to take home is likely to be accessible; and the school is locked at 5:00, meaning Ben would have to wait outside alone. It appears that Ben cannot attend the game this evening; there seem to be no possible solutions to be implemented. However, Ben's teacher, Ms. O'Malley, remembers an article in the PTA newsletter about a new 24-hour hotline for people with disabilities to increase accessible buses. Because she wants to reinforce Ben's self-determination and personal responsibility, and empower Ben's mother to build his independence, Ms. O'Malley contacts Ben's mom to suggest that Ben investigate what time he will need to get the bus on both routes and call the hotline. He has the skills to do both—if he didn't, the SDIP would suggest choosing a methodology to teach these foundational skills, perhaps direct instruction or modeling. Ben, eager to become more independent in getting around the community, decides to call the hotline and also decides to have his cell phone with him so he can call Dad in case of an emergency. A week later, Ben has created a workable option for himself; when a similar situation arises, he has no trouble taking the bus home and decides that this option will be of ongoing use to him. This shows Ben's ability to evaluate the consequence of his decisions, which fits the problem-solving methodology and the third step of the SDIP as well. The SDIP model also envisions Ben engaging in self-regulation, in which he determines if other options need to be sought for future situations, and whether he needs to learn any new foundational skills or gather additional information to be able to add new options to his repertoire.

> 66 Make sure that the parents and young adult can identify what the goals are and what the barriers could be. We recently had an employer make available a fantastic employment opportunity for a young man, a retreat in the area that functions as a lodge and meeting place for out-of-town guests and employees. He is a young man with Asperger's, very social and highly verbal. He was excited, we were excited, and they were going to hire him. Then the family examined the transportation issue. It would require 3 buses and at least an hour each way for the student, with the last part involving walking about 3 blocks with no sidewalks! Everyone was disappointed. After discussing several options, their son chose to study for his driver's license so that we can revisit this. 99
>
> *LeeAnn Wagner Cica, Postsecondary Transition Teacher, Pittsburgh, PA*

Social Skills

Social skills have been defined as a set of competencies that (a) promote positive social relationships, (b) contribute to peer acceptance and friendship development, (c) lead to satisfactory school adjustment, (d) allow students to cope with and adapt to the demands of the social environment, and (e) avoid aversive social situations (Gresham, Van & Cook, 2006; Mathur & Rutherford, 1996; Rutherford, Quinn, & Mathur, 1996). Social skills include a range of learning-related skills that allow students to study independently, work in groups, build and maintain friendships, and respond appropriately to adult feedback and correction (Gresham, Sugai, & Horner, 2001). All of these outcomes contribute to becoming more self-determined by mastering the social skills necessary to communicate one's needs in an appropriate manner and to successfully work with others to satisfy those needs. Adolescents who demonstrate positive social skills and are socially capable often experience greater academic outcomes, including increased academic engagement time (Lane et al., 2003).

The long-term implications of social skills deficits can be extremely serious. Successful employment depends largely on the ability to get along with others. In fact, deficiencies in social skills, such as lateness and inappropriate use of break time, are much more likely to cause termination of employment than are job performance factors (Jackson, Jackson, & Bennett, 1998). Social skills deficits are predictive of employment difficulties (Elksnin & Elksnin, 1998), juvenile delinquency, and mental health problems (Lo, Loe, & Cartledge, 2002) and can result in poor interpersonal development and peer and adult rejection, as well as academic failure (Kuperschmidt, Coie, & Dodge, 1990; Webb, Miller, Pierce, Strawser, & Jones, 2004).

Social skills instruction can range from teaching specific social behaviors (e.g., greeting, a nod during conversation, a handshake) that facilitate interpersonal interaction to complex behaviors such as learning formal dinner etiquette (Kerr & Nelson, 1989). In classrooms, interventions can focus on teacher-approved behaviors (e.g., raising a hand, following directions, and staying seated) or peer interaction behaviors (e.g., managing frustration, problem solving, and teamwork; Miller, Lane, & Wehby, 2005).

Gresham (1998) noted that the most effective social skills training consisted of direct teaching using modeling, coaching, and effective reinforcement. Of these components, modeling is perhaps most often used. Social skills such as cooperation, sharing, initiating positive interaction, complimenting, and many others have been taught successfully using modeling (Gresham, 1982). It is important for both teachers and parents to remember that they are role models for their students (Johns et al., 2005). How these role models treat students, and how they deal with anger, frustrating situations, or a crisis sets the tone for the classroom or the home environment. Often natural modeling can be combined with the more direct approach of coaching in building effective social skills.

For example, in seeking to help a youth develop the social skill of cooperation, the teacher or parent (functioning as a coach) would ask the child what is meant by cooperation and ask him to give specific examples of how to cooperate. Then the child would practice (perhaps through critical selection) cooperative behaviors with a peer or group of peers (e.g., working on a class play or at a family game night). The teacher or parent provides feedback and discussion on how well the child cooperated and make suggestions as to his improvement of cooperation skills. Social skills such as group participation, communicating with peers, being friendly, friendship-making skills, initiating positive interaction, and many others have been taught successfully using coaching.

However, a primary goal of social skills training is to teach students how to manage their own behavior. This means that they should become self-regulated per the SDIP, as much as possible. Young adults who are self-regulated, can evaluate options and choices and decide whether to modify existing skills or learn new ones. In essence, they judge whether their social behaviors were appropriate to the situation, and modify, enhance, or add to their repertoire if not. Although this feedback is more externally provided at the beginning of social skills instruction, it can and should become more internalized as opportunities for self-regulation increase. The SDIP can help identify problems with appropriate social behavior and establish a program to teach skills to remediate these deficits and assist the young adult in becoming a more self-determined social participant.

SCENARIO 2: SAM. Sam was diagnosed with Asperger's syndrome in the ninth grade after many years of misdiagnosis and confusion. For years he had watched other children interact without knowing how to participate; he could hold conversations with adults, who would humor him and basically let him deliver a monologue about information he had read recently. It appeared that Sam had no awareness of how it felt to be his listener.

Sam's mother worked closely with his teachers and counselors who helped her understand how the world looked through his eyes. Using the

SDIP step of identifying needed skills, they determined that Sam needed to be able to interpret facial expressions and body language; he needed to be able to understand his Asperger's syndrome, and how his typical behavior looked to others. He needed to be able to assess himself and the others during these situations and make some adjustments if it wasn't going well for the other person. Knowing how one impacts others through conversation is a critical self-determination skill.

When Sam went off topic during a conversation, his mother followed the same instructional intervention as his teachers and was able to support him to refocus on the topic by commenting that she was confused by the change in his topic. She used the concept of teachable moments to consistently relay this prompt to Sam. Over time, he was able to become more aware of those around him and their reactions to his changes in the conversation, and to use those cues to refocus the conversation to the original topic. He learned how to share himself with others and learned to internalize his own feedback system to identify external cues and alter his conversational interactions to be more socially appropriate.

Sometimes Sam will still get angry at his mother and others if they interrupt him when he's in the middle of speaking to add their comments, but then Sam can laugh about it. At some point, he may need to expand his self-regulating behaviors, per the SDIP, to seek new strategies to address overreaction, or learn how to respond to nonverbal cues others may send when he's going off-topic. At this point, though, his mother is grateful for the partnership with school practitioners and that she learned how to support him when he reverts to old "antisocial" behavior.

Participating in IEP Meetings

The special education self-determination initiative in the early 1990s, together with the implementation of IDEA regulations requiring that students be invited to the individualized education program (IEP) meeting for purposes of transition planning, led to an increase in meaningful participation of students with disabilities in the development and review their IEPs. The initiative also gave rise to efforts to promote student-led IEP meetings or *self-directed IEPs.*

Research indicates that having students lead or assist in facilitating their IEP meetings yields a higher percentage of student-selected goals incorporated in the document (Kochhar-Bryant, Bassett, & Webb, 2009). Van Reusen, Bos, Schumaker, and Deshler (1994) found student-indicated goals increased from 13% to 86% after implementation of a self-advocacy strategy for promoting student involvement in the IEP. A recent study (Martin, Van Dyke, D'Ottavio, & Nickerson, 2007) indicated that when students were present at the meeting but did not direct or facilitate it, they spoke only 3% of the time—compared to education professionals, who spoke 66% of the time.

Transition practitioners, parents, and students can work together to ensure student participation in transition planning meetings by (a) empowering them with the ability to voice preferences and suggest goals and (b) developing core procedural skills to accomplish them. This corresponds to the first stage of the SDIP, which is determining which skills should be

PRE-IEP MEETING QUESTIONS TO ELICIT STUDENT PARTICIPATION

- What are my strengths?

- How do I learn best?

- What skills do I want to learn or improve?

- Upon what vocational/career goals do I want to work?

- What kind of job would I like to have after I leave high school or college?

- What kind of living arrangement and what kind of recreation/leisure activities do I want ?

present to enable full self-determined participation. The next step is to isolate how these skills will be taught and then facilitated toward independent application.

Empowering student voice. Parents should talk with their adolescents about what they want to say, and help them phrase and practice statements before the meeting, or help write notes or an outline of what to say. Parents and teachers can use coaching as a selected instructional approach to teach students about their appropriate role in IEP meetings; they may also assist young adults by developing a series of questions to elicit information to bring to these meetings (see box, "Pre-IEP Meeting Questions to Elicit Student Participation"; Berry & Hardman, 1998).

All team members, including the parents, should know the student will be participating in the meetings and assume supportive roles. Allow for sufficient time to facilitate student participation; parents and students should reciprocate positive reinforcement for their participation in this process. James E. Martin, a national expert on student involvement in transition planning, reminds everyone that this is the student's meeting (personal communication, November 17, 2008). See box, "Promoting Student Participation and Ownership of the Process" for suggested strategies parents and practitioners can use to teach foundational skills that promote successful student participation in, and eventual ownership of, IEP and transition planning meetings (PACER, 1996; Berry & Hardman, 1998), and which include the third SDIP step, evaluation and self-regulation. Empowering the student to react to IEP team actions will strengthen the motivation to provide more information, seek more involvement (perhaps also identifying informational or skill needs to do so), and place themselves increasingly into the process.

Developing core procedural skills. Parents should make sure that their adolescents know what the IEP really is, especially that the transition section is a plan for their future. It is very important that they know that their input and options are valued by the other team members (PACER, 1996). If

PROMOTING STUDENT PARTICIPATION AND OWNERSHIP OF THE PROCESS

- Empower the student to first talk about the issues.

- Talk directly to the student.

- Ask the student questions, especially when talking about life after high school.

- Encourage parents and students to bring a list and objectives to be address at the meeting.

- Remind parents and students that they may invite others who could provide support and information. Students may want to invite friends for moral support.

- Encourage teachers not to use technical language and to avoid jargon when conveying information.

- Encourage students to ask questions; parents may be needed to assist or probe to elicit the actual concern of the student.

- Respect the time students may need to think and respond during the meeting.

- Invite students to share information relevant to transition planning.

- Make notes and integrate students' ideas and input; parents can coach students if they are having difficulty articulating the information.

- Frequently listen for and encourage students' opinions during the meeting.

- Empower the student to make changes in his/her IEP and transition plan.

- Invite students to offer feedback and reactions to the team's decisions and recommendations.

students are uncomfortable or stressful about attending the meeting, they may consider attending only part of it (PACER, 2000).

❝ In Southmoore High School in Moore, Oklahoma, special educators and parents came together to learn how to teach and support students with IEPS to become actively involved and lead their own IEP meeting. Special educators used the Self-Directed IEP instructional program to teach students how to become involved in their IEP meeting. IEP team members, including the parents, learned the students would be actively involved in leading their own meeting and how to support their students during this process. Parents, students, and special educators are pleased with the results and report an increased student level of engagement in the school process and better understanding of what they need to do to accomplish their goals. One Mom, whose son has autism, burst into tears of joy when she experienced him assuming a leadership role in his meeting and actively discussing plans for his future. Another student with autism said "I was scared at first, but once I got talking and saw that everyone listened to me I felt better. My plan is now what I want to do." When asked how this type of IEP meeting compared to what he experienced in the past, this student said "I used to just go and sit there and let them take care of everything, but not anymore." 〟

James Martin, Professor, Zarrow Center, University of Oklahoma

Kochhar-Bryant and colleagues (2009) suggest that teaching students to be more involved in the transition planning process consists of three phases: a *beginning phase,* a *during phase,* and an *after phase.* In the beginning phase, students learn how to lead or facilitate the IEP meeting; parents can assist with this by focusing on the same strategies that promote student participation. Teaching the specific process of the IEP meeting—perhaps through a combination of direct instruction, coaching, and modeling—can lead to student ownership and leadership of the process itself. Martin, Marshall, Maxon, and Jerman (1996) identified 11 steps students can follow to lead their IEP meetings:

1. Begin the meeting by stating the purpose.
2. Introduce everyone.
3. Review past goals and performance.
4. Ask for feedback from other team members.
5. State your transition goals.
6. Ask questions if you don't understand.
7. Deal with difference of opinion.
8. State what support you need.
9. Summarize your goals.
10. Close the meeting by thanking everyone for attending and sharing information.
11. Work on IEP/transition goals throughout the year.

As with empowering student voice, students should be encouraged to evaluate the procedure and what was accomplished, and suggest ways to improve the process and/or their role in it. The true intent of the SDIP is achieved if the student is able to articulate a critique, as well as indicate what skills he or she need to develop to feel more confident in leading the meeting.

Self-Advocacy/Self-Disclosure in Higher Education Settings

According to NLTS2, about three out of five youth with disabilities and their parents had expectations of some type of postsecondary education after high school as opposed to 92% of parents of peers in the general population. Students with disabilities enroll in postsecondary education at about half the rate of their peers without disabilities (Wagner, Newman, Cameto, Garza, & Levine, 2005).

Students who have participated in or led their IEP meetings will most likely have little difficulty with self-disclosing and advocating for what they need to be successful at the postsecondary level. They are already accustomed to discussing their disabilities, their learning needs, and how they learn best. The difference between high school and college is that while in high school, someone on the IEP team is responsible for systemically ensuring students get what they need, but students must assume this responsibility when they enter college.

Students with disabilities and their parents frequently believe that it is their responsibility to notify a college or university of their disability during the application process. It is not. In fact, under Section 504 of the Rehabilitation Act of 1973 and the Americans With Disabilities Act of 1990 (ADA), students with disabilities are not required to disclose that they have a disability—nor can any postsecondary institution make preadmission inquiries to determine whether an individual has a disability (HEATH Resource Center, 2006). If students do not require any accommodations, or choose not to access them, they can choose not to disclose. The NLTS2 findings indicate that more than half (52%) of youth with disabilities who received services in high school do not consider themselves to have a disability by the time they have transitioned to postsecondary school; an additional 7% consider themselves to have a disability but choose not to disclose it to their college or university. Only 40% of students with disabilities self-disclose having a disability and inform their postsecondary schools of such (Wagner et al., 2005). Parents and practitioners can guide youth through the process of considering benefits and disadvantages of disclosure, using materials like the *411 Disability Disclosure Workbook* (National Collaborative on Workforce and Disability for Youth, 2005). Per the SDIP, parents and practitioners must help students decide the type of knowledge and skills they need to seek and advocate for needed services, including (a) legal parameters for accessing services and considerations for making disclosure decisions, (b) procedures for accessing services, and (c) the appropriate use of self-determination in the process.

Legal Parameters

An institution is only required to provide academic adjustments for student disabilities of which it has been informed. In other words, any student who has been admitted to a college or university and who requires academic adjustments for a disability must disclose his or her disability and request the necessary academic adjustments through the institution's office for disability support services (DSS) or the appropriate administrator. Students who request academic adjustments for a disability must also provide current documentation of the disability. Therefore, although it is the student's choice whether or not to disclose the disability, institutions are only bound to consider requests for academic adjustments from those students who self-identify and whose documentation is complete. A similar legislative policy pertains to requesting accommodations in the work setting under the ADA. Choices regarding disclosure in the workplace can mirror those made in the higher education setting. Job-seekers may choose to disclose disability-specific information for a variety of reasons, including (a) obtaining information to assist in creating a plan to address possible barriers and accommodations, (b) identifying disability-specific services and support networks, and (c) discussing disability issues with employers to determine if the demands of the environment can be met with or without reasonable accommodations (National Collaborative on Workforce and Disability for Youth, 2005).

> ❝ My daughter has some learning difficulties that appear when she takes some subjects but not others. She just enrolled at the local community college and took 9 credits this past semester and will most likely take 12 credits next semester. Currently, she has not requested any accommodations and is doing quite well. However, she will soon need to take a math class and this is a subject where she needs some accommodations, such as extra time on tests. I spoke to her about requesting such accommodations and that this will mean self-disclosing her disabilities. She seems to be uncomfortable to do so. I am encouraging her to speak with disability support services staff and hope they can provide her with some self-advocacy skills that will help her through this process. I'm also hoping that she realizes that requesting accommodations will help her maximize her success in a difficult subject area. ❞
>
> *Hugh Berry, Parent, Baltimore, Maryland*

Procedures for Accessing Services

Individuals with disabilities who are embarking on postsecondary education should know (a) the type of disability they have (and have written documentation of their disability), (b) the laws that entitle them to protection, (c) the types of protections they qualify for under the laws, and (d) academic adjustments they may need. If students require support services and/or accommodations at the postsecondary level, they are responsible for identifying what is needed and for providing the necessary documentation about their disability. This documentation must be obtained from a professional who is qualified to assess the particular disability. This documentation must provide (a) a statement of specific disability or diagnosis and (b) a logical reason for the requested accommodations based on the limitations to learning caused by the specific disability or diagnosis. Students should be strongly encouraged to contact the school they plan to attend to learn exactly what documentation is required.

Transition practitioners should consider helping their students request that an updated evaluation be performed during their senior year. However, the school does not have to honor this request. Students should also be involved in the Summary of Performance, which should identify the accommodations necessary for success in a postsecondary setting. Again, the college or university does not have to accept this summary as documentation, but some are taking it into consideration.

Because the postsecondary school has no responsibility to recognize the parents' role in the process past the age of 18, the request for accommodation must come from the student. If students want their parents to have a role in their postsecondary education, students must invite them to do so. However, the postsecondary institution may still deal only with the student in all matters except tuition. The school, including the DSS staff, cannot discuss any student information with anyone, including their parents, without the student's permission (U.S. Department of Education, 2008).

Self-Determination in Accessing Services

Transition practitioners cannot emphasize the need for self-disclosure enough: Students must be able to self-identify and discuss their disability and needs and work with the DSS staff to obtain necessary accommodations. Students must have the self-determination skills to be a self-advocate and be willing to identify themselves as having a disability to the administrator responsible for providing accommodations and support services to students with disabilities. In addition, they very often find themselves in a position of having to advocate for themselves and their accommodation needs in the classroom with faculty.

The appropriate instructional strategies to help students develop the procedural skills related to disclosure may involve a combination of (a) direct instruction (providing access to key information sources), (b) coaching (guiding the students through the initial information-seeking outreach to desired postsecondary settings), (c) problem solving (determining how to deal with a roadblock in securing needed documentation), and (d) using teachable moments (e.g., asking for appropriate accommodations when taking the SAT). The evaluation aspect of the SDIP occurs when the young adult is able to not only determine if the processes in which they have engaged turn out in their favor, but also whether other types of procedural information are needed and where they can be accessed. Instructional approaches for teaching self-advocacy itself in this context can mirror those used for teaching procedural knowledge and skill sets. Once students understand the parameters of disclosure, as well as what legally can be provided in the postsecondary setting, their actual capacity to approach faculty and staff will rest in their confidence to voice needs and their clarity of expression. Perhaps guidance counselors can be helpful in facilitating the development of these skills, especially if students are uncomfortable and reluctant to discuss their disabilities.

Finally, youth with disabilities should be facilitated as they monitor the success or failure of support services and feel empowered to seek adjustments to support patterns. Considering that parents may no longer intervene on students' behalf without their express permission, it is essential that young adults with disabilities engage in constant evaluation of services, identify areas that require change, and own the self-advocacy needed to pursue it.

Skills Parents Need to Develop, and How Practitioners Can Help

Ultimately, there are several overarching skills parents need in order to support their adolescent's emergent independence across adult domains

TIPS FOR PARENTS

- Encourage students to make choices, set priorities, and make decisions about everyday activities such as what to wear, what foods to eat during snacks, and so forth.

- Illustrate to students that choices have results or consequences that need to be considered. For example, "If I choose a candy bar at every snack, I will not be eating in a healthy way," or "If I choose the same shirt to wear daily, it will be dirty most days."

- Help students to identify interests, strengths, and needs, and to understand that these characteristics are part of who they are.

- Explain to students that a goal is something that they want to achieve, and that barriers are things that may get in the way of achieving goals. Encourage them to assess whether they need to learn something new, change something in the environment, or both to overcome the barriers.

- Use questions to support the process of logical problem solving. As students become more familiar with the process, parents can let them lead problem-solving discussions.

- Place students at the center of goal setting, action planning, and progress monitoring—even if they require extensive support to complete these activities.

- Let students decide on a schedule and action plan, as well as monitor their own progress.

- Support students' need to rethink a goal, if progress is slow or minimal. Encourage them to adjust or rework the action plan, if they want to pursue the goal.

- At the end of the process, be sure to ask how the student felt about the goal and what he or she learned.

(see box, "Tips for Parents"; Lee et al., 2006). These skills enable parents to teach their children from an early age to make good choices and set appropriate goals.

Practitioners who are sensitive to the unique characteristics of each family will recognize individual differences and the importance of engaging in ongoing dialogue with parents about these needs and the supports they require. See box, "Tips for Practitioners" for a few examples of how schools can support parents in the process of support student learning and development (Brandes, 2005; Massachusetts Department of Education, 2000).

Parents and transition practitioners teach students many important skills. Although they may focus on different skill sets, often parents' and teachers' efforts target the same skill or behavior. Research has indicated that the student's level of skill mastery will increase if teachers and parents

TIPS FOR PRACTITIONERS

- Inform parents about curricular goals and assessments for students in each subject at each grade level and suggest ways to complement the curriculum in the home environment.

- Inform parents of homework expectations and policies, including information about how to best assist students with assignments.

- Provide opportunities for parents to learn about differences in how students learn (learning styles, multiple intelligences, etc.) and prepare for school (studying, motivation, test preparation, etc.).

- Involve family members in setting goals for students, making course selections, determining IEP goals, and planning for transition to postsecondary education, careers, and the workplace.

- Provide opportunities for parents to learn how they can effectively support their student's education.

- Demonstrate ways to reinforce behaviors at home that enhance learning, such as time management, organizational skills, planning, and limited television viewing and computer use.

- Encourage parents to model good reading habits, participate in informal educational activities in the home and community, and promote lifelong learning.

- Engage parents in discussion and pay attention to the issues they bring up.

- Invite parents to share goals for their child; they are members of the planning team.

- Share expertise and resources with parents, offering any information that may be beneficial such as brochures or Web sites on vocational rehabilitation services.

- Share the relevance of the curriculum to the student's goals. This may be particularly important in regard to self-determination, a concept parents may not be familiar with and view as a bit intimidating.

- State expectations early and regularly. Parents can be supportive only when they understand exactly what is expected of their child.

- Appreciate parents' support and follow-through at home. Be specific about the positive impact their efforts are having on their child's progress in school.

work collaboratively (Henderson & Mapp, 2002; Patrikakou, 2004). Although such collaboration is important, students too must become integral partners in this collaboration as they reach transition age and assume more independence and responsibility for themselves; this is the ultimate goal of education and requires a concerted effort by teachers and parents to develop necessary self-determination skills.

INDICATORS OF SUCCESS FOR EMPOWERING PARENTS AS INSTRUCTORS OF THEIR YOUTH'S EMERGENT INDEPENDENCE

○ Parents support their youth's development of self-determination skills in school and provide them with opportunities practice these skills at home and in the community.

○ Parents have been provided information and support in developing their own skills to instruct their youth using the SDIP model (identifying skills, determining instructional method, and engaging in evaluation and self-regulation).

○ Parents and teachers collaboratively prepare youth to participate fully in or lead their own IEP meetings.

○ Parents assist their youth in understanding their disabilities and requesting the necessary accommodations to be successful in postsecondary education and employment.

REFERENCES

Agran, M., Wehmeyer, M. L., Cavin, M., & Palmer, S. (2008). Promoting student active classroom participation skills through instruction to promote self-regulated learning and self-determination. *Career Development for Exceptional Individuals, 31,* 106–114.

Berry, J. O., & Hardman, M. L. (1998). *Lifespan perspectives on the family and disability.* Boston: Allyn & Bacon.

Brandes, J. A. (2005). Partner with parents. *Intervention in School & Clinic, 41,* 52–54.

Caplan, J., Hall, G., Lubin, S., & Fleming, R. (1997). *Parent involvement: Literature review of school-family partnerships.* Oak Brook, IL: North Central Regional Educational Laboratory.

Carr, J. F., Herman, N., & Harris, D. E. (2005). *Creating dynamic schools through mentoring, coaching, and collaboration.* Alexandria, VA: Association for Supervision and Curriculum Development.

Carter, S. (2003). *Educating our children together: A sourcebook for effective family-school-community partnerships.* Albany, NY: Consortium for Appropriate Dispute Resolution in Special Education (CADRE) and New York State Education Department.

Cleaver, S. (2008, November/December). Meet the micro-managers. *Instructor, 118*(3), 30–36.

Cook, C. C., Brotherson, M. J., Weigel-Garrey, C., & Mize, I. (1996). Homes to support the self-determination of children. In D. J. Sands & M. L. Wehmeyer (Eds.), *Self-determination across the life span: Independence and choice for people with disabilities* (pp. 91–110). Baltimore: Paul H. Brookes.

Crowe, C. (2008). Solving behavior problems together. *Educational Leadership, 66*(3), 44–47.

Damast, A. (2007, April 17). Invasion of the helicopter parents. *Business Week Online,* p. 4.

Doll, B., Sands, D. J., Wehmeyer, M. L., & Palmer, S. (1996). Promoting the development and acquisition of self-determined behavior. In D. J. Sands & M. L. Wehmeyer (Eds.), *Self-determination across the life span: Independence and choice for people with disabilities* (pp. 63–88). Baltimore, MD: Paul H. Brookes.

Elksnin, L. K., & Elksnin, N. (1998). *Assessment and instruction of social skills.* San Diego, CA: Singular.

Elliott, S., & Gresham, F. M. (1991). *Social skills intervention guide.* Circle Pines, MN: American Guidance.

Epstein, J. L. (2001). *School, family, and community partnerships: Preparing educators and improving schools.* Boulder, CO: Westview Press.

Field, S., Hoffman, A., & Posch, M. (1997). Self-determination during adolescence: A developmental perspective. *Remedial and Special Education, 18,* 285–293.

Field, S., Martin, J., Miller, R., Ward, M., & Wehmeyer, M. (1998). *A practical guide to teaching self-determination.* Reston, VA: Council for Exceptional Children.

Gresham, F. (1982). Social skills instruction for exceptional children. *Theory into Practice, 21,* 129–133.

Gresham, F. M. (1998). Designs for evaluating behavior change: Conceptual principles of single case methodology. In T. S. Watson & F. M. Gresham (Eds.), *Handbook of child behavior therapy* (pp. 23–40). New York: Plenum.

Gresham, F. M., Sugai, G., & Horner, R. H. (2001). Interpreting outcomes of social skills training for students with high-incidence disabilities. *Exceptional Children, 67,* 331–344.

Gresham, F. M., Van, M. B., & Cook, C. R. (2006). Social skills training for teaching replacement behaviors: Remediating acquisition deficits in at-risk students. *Behavioral Disorders, 31,* 363–377.

Grigal, M., Neubert, D. A., Moon, M. S., & Graham, S. (2003). Self-determination for students with disabilities: Views of parents and teachers. *Exceptional Children, 70,* 97–112.

Guskey T. R., & Andermanm, E. M. (2008). Students at bat. *Educational Leadership, 66*(3), 8–14.

Halloran, W. D. (1993). Transition services requirement: Issues, implications, challenge. In R. C. Eaves & P. J. McLaughlin (Eds.), *Recent advances in special education and rehabilitation* (pp. 210–224). Boston: Andover.

HEATH Resource Center. (2006). *Guidance and career counselors' toolkit: Advising high school students with disabilities on postsecondary options.* Washington, DC: Author.

Henderson, A. T., & Mapp, K. L. (2002) *A new wave of evidence: The impact of school family, and community connections on student achievement.* Annual synthesis, 2002. Austin, TX: National Center for Family and Community Connections with Schools. (ERIC Document Reproduction Service No. ED474521)

Hoover-Dempsey, K. V., & Sandler, H. M. (1995). Parents' reported involvement in students' homework: Strategies and practices. *Elementary School Journal, 95,* 435–450.

Jackson, D. A., Jackson, N. F., & Bennett, M. I. (1998). *Teaching social competence to youth and adults with developmental disabilities.* Austin: Pro-Ed.

Johns, B. H., Crowley, E. P., & Guetzloe, E. (2005). The central role of teaching social skills. *Focus on Exceptional Children, 37*(8), 1–8.

Kerr, M. M., & Nelson, C. M. (1989). *Strategies for managing behavior problem in the classroom* (2nd ed.). Columbus, OH: Merrill.

Kochhar-Bryant, C., Basset, D. S., & Webb, K. W. (2009). *Transition to postsecondary education for students with disabilities.* Thousand Oaks, CA: Corwin Press.

Kochhar-Bryant, C., & Greene, G. (2009). *Pathways to successful transition for youth with disabilities: A developmental process.* Upper Saddle River, NJ: Merrill.

Kuperschmidt, J., Coie, J., & Dodge, K. (1990). The role of peer relationships in the development of disorders. In S. Asher & J. Coie (Eds.), *Peer rejection in childhood* (pp. 274–308). New York: Cambridge University Press.

Lane, K. L., Wehby, J., Menzies, H. H., Doukas, G. L., Muntont, S. M., & Gregg, R. M. (2003). Social skills instruction for students at risk for antisocial behavior: The effects of small-group instruction. *Behavioral Disorders, 28,* 229–248.

Lee, S. H., Palmer, S. B., Turnbull, A. P., & Wehmeyer, M. L. (2006). A model for parent-teacher collaboration to promote self-determination in young children with disabilities. *TEACHING Exceptional Children, 38*(3), 36–41.

Lo, Y., Loe, S. A., & Cartledge, G. (2002). The effects of social skills instruction on the social behaviors of students at risk for emotional or behavioral disorders. *Behavioral Disorders, 27,* 371–385.

Martin, J. E., Marshall, L. H., Maxon, L. M., & Jerman P. L. (1996). *The self-directed IEP.* Longmont, CO: Sopris West.

Martin, J. E., Van Dyke, J., D'Ottavio, M., & Nickerson, K. (2007). The student-directed Summary of Performance: Increasing student and family involvement in the transition planning process. *Career Development for Exceptional Individuals, 30,* 13-26.

Massachusetts Department of Education. (2000). *The parent, family, and community involvement guide.* Malden, MA: Author.

Mathur, S., & Rutherford, R. (1996). Is social skills training effective for students with emotional or behavioral disorders? Research issues and needs. *Behavioral Disorders, 22,* 21–27.

Miller, M. J., Lane, K. L,, & Wehby, J. (2005). Social skills instruction for students with high-incidence disabilities: a school-based intervention to address acquisition deficits. *Preventing School Failure, 49,* 27–39.

National Collaborative on Workforce and Disability for Youth. (2005). *The 411 on disability disclosure workbook.* Washington, DC: Institute for Educational Leadership.

O'Shea, D. J., O'Shea, L. J., Algozzine, R., & Hammitte, D. J. (2001). *Families and teachers of individuals with disabilities: Collaborative orientations and responsive practices.* Boston: Allyn & Bacon.

PACER Center. (1996). *IEP: Involving the student is important for a successful plan.* (Action Information Sheet: PHP-c6). Minneapolis, MN: Author.

PACER Center. (2000). *How can my child be involved in the IEP process?* (Action Information Sheet: PHP-c77). Minneapolis, MN: Author.

Patrikakou, E. N. (2004). *Adolescence: Are parents relevant to students' high school achievement and post-secondary attainment?* Cambridge. MA: Harvard Family Research Project. Retrieved September 25, 2008, from http://www.hfrp.org/publications-resources/browse-our-publications/adolescence-are-parents-relevant-to-students-high-school-achievement-and-post-secondary-attainment

Perske, R. (1972). The dignity of risk. In W. Wolfensberger (Ed.), *Normalization: The principle of normalization in human services* (pp. 194–200). Toronto: National Institute on Mental Retardation.

Rockwell, R. E., Andrew, L. C., & Hawley, M. K. (1996). *Parents and teachers as partners: Issues and challenges.* Orlando: Harcourt Brace & Company.

Rutherford, R., Quinn, M., & Mathur, S. (1996). *Effective strategies for teaching appropriate behaviors to children with emotional/behavioral disorders.* Reston, VA: Council for Children with Behavioral Disorders.

San Diego City Schools. (1991). *Educators' assumptions that hinder or facilitate home-school collaboration.* San Diego: Author.

Sulzer-Azaroff, B., & Mayer, R. (1991). *Behavior analysis for lasting change.* Ft. Worth, TX: Harcourt Brace College.

Tomlison, C. A. (2008). Differentiation creates conditions for students to willingly take charge of their own learning. *Educational Leadership, 66*(3), 26–30.

U.S. Department of Education. *Family Educational Rights and Privacy Act (FERPA).* Retrieved December 30, 2008, from http://www.ed.gov/policy/gen/guid/fpco/ferpa/index.html

Van Reusen, A. K., Bos, C. S., Schumaker, J. B., & Deshler, D. D. (1994). *The self-advocacy strategy.* Lawrence, KS: Edge Enterprises.

Vaughn, S., Bos, C., & Schumm, J. S. (1997). *Teaching mainstreamed, diverse, and at-risk students in the general education classroom.* Boston: Allyn & Bacon.

Wagner, M., Newman, L., Cameto, R., Garza, N., & Levine, P. (2005). *After high school: A first look at the postschool experiences of youth with disabilities.* A report from the National Longitudinal Transition Study-2 (NLTS2) Menlo Park, CA: SRI International. Available at www.nlts2.org/reports/2005_04/nlts2_report_2005_04_complete.pdf

Ward, M. J. (1996). Coming of age in the age of self-determination: A historical perspective on self-determination. In D. Sands & M. L. Wehmeyer (Eds.), *Self-determination across the life span: Theory and practice.* Baltimore, MD: Paul H. Brookes.

Ward, M. J., & Kohler, P. D. (1996). Promoting self-determination for individuals with disabilities: Content and process. In L. E. Powers, G. H. S. Singer, & J. Sowers (Eds.), *Making our way: Building self-competence among children with disabilities.* Baltimore: Paul H. Brookes.

Webb, B. J., Miller, S. P., Pierce, T. B., Strawser, S., & Jones, W. P. (2004). Effects of social skill instruction for high-functioning adolescents with autism spectrum disorders. *Focus on Autism and Other Developmental Disabilities, 19,* 53–62.

Webster-Stratton, C., Reid, M. J., & Hammond, M. (2001). Preventing conduct problems, promoting social competence: A parent and teacher training partnership in Head Start. *Journal of Clinical Child Psychology, 30,* 283–302.

Wehmeyer, M. L. (1999). A functional model of self-determination: Describing development and implementing instruction. *Focus on Autism and Other Developmental Disabilities, 14,* 53–61.

Wehmeyer, M. L., Hughes, C., Agran, M., Garner, N., & Yeager, D. (2003). Self-directed learning strategies to promote the progress of students with intellectual disability in inclusive classrooms. *International Journal of Inclusive Education, 7,* 415–428.

Wehmeyer, M. L., Morningstar, M., & Husted, D. (1999). *Family involvement in transition planning and implementation.* Austin, TX: Pro-Ed.

Wehmeyer, M. L., Palmer, S., Agran, M., Mithaug, D., & Martin, J. (2000). Promoting causal agency: The self-determined learning model of instruction. *Exceptional Children, 66,* 439–453.

Wolery, M., & Lane, K. (2005). *Responding to children's behavior and play.* Unpublished manuscript, Vanderbilt University, Nashville, TN.

Wolfendale, S. (2002, October). *Standard-bearing: Assuring quality in parent partnership services.* Paper presented at the National Network of Parent Partnership Services Conference, Birmingham, England.

Zhang, D. (2005). Parent practices in facilitating self-determination skills: The influences of culture, socioeconomic status, and children's special education status. *Research & Practice for Persons with Severe Disabilities, 30*(3), 154–162.

Zhang, D., Katsiyannis, A., & Zhang, J. (2002). Teacher and parent practice on fostering self-determination of high school students with mild disabilities. *Career Development for Exceptional Individuals, 25,* 157–169.

Zhang, D., Wehmeyer, M. L., & Chen, L. J. (2005). Parent and teacher engagement in fostering self-determination in students with disabilities: A comparison between the U.S. and the R.O.C. *Remedial and Special Education, 26,* 55–64.

ABOUT THE AUTHOR

MICHAEL J. WARD currently coordinates the Transition Special Education Distance Education Certificate Program at George Washington University. From 1987 to 1997, he administered the Secondary Education and Transitional Services Branch in the U.S. Office of Special Education Programs and conceived a funding priority to teach skills necessary for self-determination to youth with disabilities. Evidence of this initiative is in practice today with the expansion of student-led individualized education programs and their increased decision making in career choices and attending postsecondary education.

5

Parents as Evaluators and Decision Makers

Cherie Takemoto and Cathy Healy

ESSENTIAL QUESTIONS

○ What are the critical opportunities and challenges for parents' engagement as evaluators and decision makers, as it relates to transition, at both individual child-based and systemic levels?

○ What are the prerequisite skills and knowledge that practitioners need to energize this parental role?

○ What strategies can be used to assimilate parents into this role?

When the Individuals With Disabilities Education Improvement Act (IDEA) was reauthorized in 2004, Congress made it clear that special education services are intended to lead to positive outcomes after high school and that challenging expectations will help prepare students with disabilities to lead productive and independent lives. Researchers have established a link between positive student outcomes and strategically planned parent involvement practices (Epstein, Sanders & Sheldon, 2007; Sheldon & Epstein, 2005). In the spirit of parent partnerships articulated in IDEA, school practitioners should look for a variety of ways to engage parents in the various roles delineated in this book. This chapter focuses on valuing parents as evaluators and decision makers on behalf of their children, and the systems that serve them on a continuous basis.

According to *Merriam-Webster Online* (2008), *evaluation* is "the act of determining the significance, worth, or condition of, usually by careful appraisal and study" and *deciding* is "the determination arrived at after consideration." These definitions connote a process that is investigatory, predicated on information gathering, and includes weighing variables and coming to conclusions. It is reasonable to assume that parents generally will make decisions based on personal experience, family cultural values, economic circumstance, and family education levels. Although these are important factors to be considered, they are an insufficient basis for the level of parental evaluation and decision making that fully evolved home–school partnership implies. When the opportunities of this distinct role are fully understood, practitioners will endeavor to create a climate of trust and openness so that parents are empowered to emerge as shared owners in evaluation and decision making.

Parents as Evaluators and Decision Makers in Their Child's Education Program

Legal Foundations

The No Child Left Behind Act of 2001 (NCLB) required schools and districts to be accountable to the community and especially parents, in three ways. First, they were required to report student achievement on state achievement tests and use stakeholder groups for self-evaluation and planning for improvement on the basis of making adequate yearly progress (AYP). Local school systems report AYP data, disaggregated for subgroups of race, free/reduced-price lunch, English language learners, and special education. These data are reported to the public, and school report cards are sent to parents so that they will know how their child's school is performing. Second, NCLB included school choice provisions for families whose children are attending low performing schools. Schools not meeting AYP must inform parents of their school choice rights and other school options. Third, NCLB required that parents be notified if their children receive instruction from teachers who are not "highly qualified." This provision, was another factor that contributed to the increase in inclusion of secondary students receiving special education services into general education classrooms, where they would be taught by highly qualified general education teachers (*Roundtable Discussion,* 2005).

This shift in service environment was further supported by outcomes data from the National Longitudinal Transition Study Wave 2 (NLTS2), which indicate that students with disabilities who had been educated in the general education classroom were more likely to be employed or to participate in further education after graduation (Wagner, Newman, Cameto, Levine, & Garza, 2006). For many students and their parents, contemplating the decision to move from a protected special education classroom to a general education classroom could raise fears of the unknown. Practitioners who support strong youth outcomes can help parents embrace this challenge by encouraging them to engage general education faculty and adult service providers as partners and not rely solely on communication with special education case managers. School systems, in partnership with parents, can support general education teachers who may be content-rich but short on strategies and resources to serve the unique needs of students with disabilities to further enhance achievement for all students. Discussions about school and classroom choice give parents and youth opportunities to constructively critique service provision and express their opinions about its appropriateness for the individual student.

NCLB requires that all parents be given opportunities to evaluate the effectiveness of their local school in meeting the learning needs of their children in these three ways; IDEA provides parents of transitioning youth with disabilities many more opportunities for evaluation and decision making. These opportunities are ensured by the state Procedural Safeguards documents disseminated to each parent within the special education process. IDEA gives parents rights to critique the delivery of services, and specific procedures to voice their disagreement if they believe their rights or their child's rights were violated. Schools cannot assess nor provide special education services without parent informed participation and consent. But do parents really understand the significance of their evaluative and decision-making power?

> ❝ For a long time we had always heard that of our two middle schools, Hammond had a better track record. We wanted to keep our son in his neighborhood school with his peers, but had we known Hammond had higher test scores in reading and math we probably would have pushed the IEP team to make a recommendation to have him attend that middle school. ❞
>
> *A parent*

Implications for Practitioner Actions

Within each youth's individualized education program (IEP), transition practitioners in partnership with parents and especially youth themselves must develop individual transition plans that are results-oriented and outcome-based. During these discussions, parents should be encouraged to critically appraise various options and contribute to consideration of alternatives. Practice in evaluation and decision making during the IEP planning process will prepare parents for an empowered stance during secondary transition planning, when families must consider unfamiliar service patterns and providers.

Families want what practitioners want. They want to see that their hopes, dreams, and hard work lead to meaningful and successful lives for their children. Families in a partnership role provide valuable expertise to transition practitioners as transition plans are developed and incorporated into the IEP. Families provide insight and inspiration in decisions about postsecondary goals. More important, they contribute their perspectives about what is working from a "whole-child" perspective. When the IEP team evaluates the youth's progress on the IEP towards postsecondary goals, the parents' observational contributions add a real life/real world perspective on the effectiveness of instructional and experiential components of the IEP. Further, parents can supply information about community-based opportunities that enrich and extend their young adult's learning beyond the confines of the school. Parents' situational experiences can bring a depth and range of information and questions useful in collaboratively evaluating the appropriateness of services for the individual child (see box, Representative Questions About the Appropriateness of Services").

Despite the clear benefits of parent evaluative questioning throughout the K to 12 years and beyond, such involvement appears not to sustain itself throughout that time span. Home–school partnerships begin in early

REPRESENTATIVE QUESTIONS ABOUT THE APPROPRIATENESS OF SERVICES

- How can your program address my child's problem with managing time?

- How will that career program give my child extra support in improving his reading to the level he will need for that career?

- Why is she being offered job-shadowing opportunities in fields outside of her interests?

- Does your program provide travel training so she can get to her job safely?

childhood education with active and engaged participation, especially because many special education and related services are provided in the home through individualized family service plans. Parent ownership peaks during elementary school and frequently wanes as the student enters middle school and exercises an increasing desire for autonomy (Kreider, Caspe, Kennedy, & Weiss, 2007). Adolescents in middle school, as a natural developmental progression, want to act independently but still need parental oversight; parental involvement in the transition planning process still remains a strong indicator of outcomes (Kochhar-Bryant & Greene, 2009). Distinct adolescent developmental stages that reflect this growing autonomy, starting at ages 12 to 14, include increasingly strong influences of peer groups, emotional and eventual physical distance from parents, self-discovery, career focus, and self-sustaining living (Kochhar-Bryant & Greene). This transformational time coincides precisely with the timing for the beginning of mandated transition planning. At this point, parents can be reempowered as partners by practitioners who ask probing questions and support parents to do the same. It should be recognized that stepping into a shared decision-making role is difficult for many families when they may have assumed a less active role in the IEP process.

NLTS2 data contained mixed findings about parent involvement during the transition years. Generally, parents reported satisfaction with their involvement in IEP planning, but about a third of parents wished they were more involved. At the same time, NLTS2 found a decrease in the percentage of parents who attended IEP meetings when transition was discussed (Wagner et al., 2006). On the surface, these data support the commonly held belief that parents simply become less involved in their children's education as children progress into secondary school, yet the National Network of Partnership Schools' research found that parent involvement at the secondary level can be just as frequent as in elementary years if parent engagement activities are strategically planned to address the issues for parents at that stage (Epstein, 2005). Once again, if parents are not engaged, they will lose opportunities to practice being constructively critical consumers of services for their children and youth.

" Mrs. S sensed the frustration of Michael, her 18-year old-son with Down syndrome. He was bored with the offerings of the community-based instructional program, as he had been out in the community for years making his own purchases at the local convenience store and taking karate classes with the regular parks and recreation program. Mrs. S believed that a real job in the community would be far more interesting and relevant than the simulated work experiences offered by the school. At the IEP meeting, Michael and his mother requested that the employment specialist find Michael a job to provide him with interaction with the typically developing population, require him to develop job readiness skills, and create a work history that would be needed if future employment was to be realized. Although the school usually didn't coordinate work experience for students in his program until after they turned 19, they agreed and helped Michael secure a part-time position at the local grocery store. He left high school with an IEP diploma a year before his eligibility expired and 3 years later he continues to be employed in a job for 20 hours a week. He has been found eligible for Social Security disability income and most recently Medicare. 〝

Challenges to Reciprocal Decision Making and Evaluation

For more than 30 years the Parent Educational Advocacy Training Center (PEATC) has listened to the stories of families and practitioners as they struggle to form equal and respectful partnerships with schools so that children with disabilities can reach their full potential. We have learned in our daily interactions with culturally, linguistically, socioeconomically, and geographically diverse families and have heard from many practitioners about what it takes to truly engage in collaborative decision making. We believe that there are four key challenges in empowering parents as evaluators and decision makers in their children's programs.

First, practitioners must *establish an environment of trust and safety* in which concerns and issues are heard, valued, and are an integral part of planning discussions for the youth's program. Parents who have assumed more passive roles from years of meetings that focused on compliance rather than personalized responsiveness will need to be assured that their critical questions and appraisal of options make valued contributions to transition-related decisions. Practitioners may need to recognize instances where a family's cultural mores would prohibit them from asking critical questions of perceived authority figures and establish alternate strategies to solicit these parents' unspoken concerns.

A second challenge is to *value parents as informed experts.* But what does this really mean? Many parents, through years of consultation with medical or therapeutic specialists, have developed an early and extensive expertise that should be shared with the school/agency practitioners who are newly working with their child with more significant disabilities. On the other hand, parents of youth with high-incidence disabilities such as learning disabilities, attention deficit hyperactivity disorders, mild emotional/behavioral disorders, or mild developmental disabilities—which are typically not diagnosed until school age—may have little understanding of the specific ramifications of their child's disability because a school professional has never stopped to explain it in parent-friendly terms. What does an auditory processing deficit mean? How would a visual integration disorder impact their child's learning? What strategies can assist a student with attention difficulties? If parents are to support their adolescents to become self-advocates, they must first understand these terms themselves and learn from professionals how to support their children to use learning strategies effectively. Because parents will continue as a lifelong support in the youth's own self-evaluation of what's working and decision making at critical life junctures, they will indeed need to be an empowered expert voice on their child.

Third, *parents may be confused about where to seek information* about options. They may be challenged by a lack of a single point of contact (e.g., multiple case managers) from which information can be sought (Schoeller & Emanuel, 2003). When parents need to ask investigatory questions to evaluate the appropriateness of their youth's program, and that child is served by multiple providers (often in different systems), it is confusing, frustrating, and exhausting to identify knowledgeable sources for targeted information.

The fourth challenge is dealing with *disagreements between parent and practitioner.* Can practitioners still regard parents as the expert on their child when they disagree with the more "experienced" recommendations of transition professionals? When everyone agrees, collaboration is easy. However, how can transition practitioners support parent decision making when parents disagree with them? Transition practitioners are often perplexed by responses from families when the responses are in direct contrast to what is thought to be a positive outcome for a student. Sometimes parents disagree with practitioners because they are missing critical information about options; sometimes the disagreement may stem from parents who possess critical information that conflicts with the practitioner-proposed options.

The following scenario further illustrates the power of practitioners listening to the parent's questions and identifying not only information she needed, but also valuing new information she offered, as an integral part of the service decision-making process. The school invited Mrs. M and Roberto (age 16) to an IEP team meeting to discuss his lack of progress (failing grades) and their concerns that he had been talking about dropping out of school. When invited to share her thoughts about Roberto's progress, Mrs. M emphasized her desire for Roberto to graduate and then attend community college—but Roberto wanted to drop out. He saw no point in staying in school. The special educator noted that Roberto was significantly below grade level in reading, and Mrs. M asked why the school didn't offer a reading class. The discussion turned to Roberto's diagnosed visual processing learning disability and how it interfered with his learning, especially reading.

Mrs. M remarked that no one had ever explained his disability to her; she asked, "You are the teachers. What can you do to help my boy learn to read better? We will help at home. We went to an open house at the community college, and Roberto wants to go into the auto mechanics certificate program there. His father and I think this will give him good job opportunities." Together, they mapped out Roberto's options: (a) staying in high school, making up three failed courses to earn his diploma; (b) attending an alternative program that provided individualized academic skill building to prepare for the GED, as well as career exploration activities; or (c) dropping out and taking the GED test on his own. All three paths could lead to the community college mechanics certificate. Then they discussed assistive technology that could help Roberto listen to text while reading along. This technology would be available at the community college, and the special educator invited Roberto to stay after school the following Monday to try it out.

Ultimately, the team and Mrs. M left the decision up to Roberto, but now he could make an informed choice. When he realized that costs would be associated with the alternative GED program and that he would not qualify for his mother's medical insurance if he dropped out, he decided to remain in school to finish his high school diploma. The possibilities of the assistive technology gave him new hope about keeping up in his classes.

Listen to the unspoken voice. It is important to remember that parents emerge at different levels of proactivity in the evaluative process. Some may take the initiative to seek information and actively question the appropriateness of programs options. Others may have a sense of discomfort with an option, but not have the information or confidence needed to articulate their concerns or ask key questions that reflect their concerns. An effective practitioner will be sensitive to and honor the parent's level of involvement in the evaluative role and seek ways to discover parents' questions and concerns and, most important, empower them to expand their skills as critical consumers of services. As parents develop more skill in evaluative and decision-making roles, they in turn can support the self-determination and emerging independence of their youth by encouraging them to ask questions and seek alternative solutions (e.g., within the IEP or Individualized Plan for Employment development).

Table 1 presents some situations where parents may oppose practitioners' points of view and the possible underlying, unspoken reasons for that opposition. Because parents may not voice concerns or questions, practitioners who ask questions and listen to responses can bridge different perspectives and priorities between parents and transition staff. Strategically starting that conversation may build trust, demonstrate value of the parent as an expert in their child, provide a channel for information, and encourage critical discussion of differences. This, is turn, may pave the way for parents to initiate critical conversations in future encounters.

Strategies to Support Parents

Practitioners who appreciate how much more effective parents can become if they are full partners in evaluating services and programs for their young adults will incorporate strategies into parent engagement practices to support parents as they assimilate into this role. These practices address the four challenges discussed earlier. Three of these challenges can be accomplished simply by taking an intentional stance and looking for opportunities to support parents when they are apparently struggling with (a) establishing trust; (b) sharing or developing their own expertise in their child's disability, strengths, and issues; and (c) critically questioning and appraising proposed services, programs, and options. Sensitive communication from an aware practitioner can provide intangible differences in the parent's view of the school or agency that result in greater parent engagement in the evaluative component of the IEP process. The remaining challenge will need to be addressed on a more systemic level. To participate as

TABLE 1: Possible Factors Behind Parent Opposition

Parent Opposition	Possible Factors
Parent is resistant to work experience encouraged by practitioners.	Parent is worried that daughter would be exposed to men who might take advantage of her.
Parent doesn't acknowledge intensity of her son's autism spectrum disorder behaviors and how they will be an impediment to employment.	Parent has seen son working in their landscaping business where he can focus on planting, weeding, and mulching without evidence of negative behaviors.
Parent refuses to sign authorization to share info with other agencies.	Parent has a history of working with social service agencies and is mistrustful that other agencies will "interfere" in child's transition plan.
Parent doesn't agree about student potential.	Parent's cultural views of disability and limited information about services and support have led him to assume that his son will be dependent on him for life.
Parent pushes for academic program while practitioner believes functional skills are more important.	The family has a strong value on education and is investigating "alternative" postsecondary education programs. The extra push for academics will help the student's academic readiness in the alternative nondegree postsecondary experience.
Parent does not want child to work.	Family's cultural views do not include outside employment but rather see the student contributing to the family through a role in the family business.
Parent's job expectation is higher than practitioner believes is realistic for child with developmental disabilities.	Through a support network, parent associates with families whose young adult children with developmental disabilities work in traditionally "white-collar" jobs.
Parent expresses fear during discussion about self-determination.	The culture of the family is such that young people must always be respectful of the family and consider the needs of the family first before individual goals or desires.
Parent wants assistive technology that the practitioner believes would not be appropriate.	Parent has learned that other families have been able to receive assistive technology and believes the practitioner's unwillingness to help her access the technology is racially motivated.
Student says he wants something, but it is against his parent's wishes.	Parent knows of a long series of son's "bad" choices that have managed to get him into serious trouble. The parent is not willing to let her son make another wrong choice that will create even more difficulties for the family.

QUESTIONS ABOUT SCHOOL QUALITY

- How well does your child's school perform?

- How does your child's school spend money?

- Who can teach your children?

- Do parents in your district have a choice?

- Do you and your child feel comfortable at your child's school?

(Center for Education Reform, 2008)

partners in decision making, parents need to know transition mandates, procedures, and practices. They need information about in-school, community, and postschool options. They need to know about self-determination and age of majority and how these will shift coming discussions about their emergent adult. It may be more efficient for practitioners to provide needed information to groups of parents rather than one-on-one.

There are a number of Web sites aimed at empowering parents to become strong proponents of school improvement. For example, the Center for Education Reform, a public nonprofit corporation founded in 1993 in Washington, DC, asserts that it "drives the creation of better educational opportunities for all children by leading parents, policymakers and the media in boldly advocating for school choice, advancing the charter school movement, and challenging the education establishment" (2008). Its Web site urges parents to ask a series of questions (see box, "Questions About School Quality") so that they will have the broad based knowledge necessary to accurately evaluate their child's school.

Increasingly, localities have established parent information-sharing activities focused on the transition years. Many school communities organize transition evenings that parallel the activities of "college nights." Transition professionals, adult service agencies, and postsecondary education programs are invited to present an overview of their offerings to families. Other communities organize "field trips" for students and parents during the school day to visit adult programs facilitating learning and relationship building. Still other communities offer local, regional, and statewide transition conferences in which parents, professionals, and youth can network and become acquainted with the adult world. Often these parent information sessions are sponsored by parent information and training centers, funded by the federal, state, or local jurisdictions. Whatever is scheduled, practitioners need to disseminate invitations to parents, including those whose children are approaching the transition years. It is never too early to become informed (and forewarned) about issues they will soon be facing with their young adolescents. In advance of or during these information-sharing activities, it is suggested that a list of "frequently asked questions" be disseminated; this will engage parents in knowing what questions to ask when a service option presents itself, which is the foundation to helping them develop their own set of questions they can use to evaluate other options they may encounter. This type of resource also can be used to introduce their youth with a disability to the idea of critically approaching service opportunities with the intent of making informed evaluation-based choices.

INDICATORS OF SUCCESS FOR EFFECTIVE SERVICE EVALUATORS AND DECISION MAKERS

○ The parent responds to the environment of trust and respect established by practitioners.

○ The parent has critical information about the youth's disability and how it may impact the youth's current and future functioning.

○ The parent has basic understanding of transition planning and its significance.

○ The parent has information and ideas about what happens when special education ends, including postsecondary service options for which their child may be eligible.

○ The parent is able to identify viable sources of information and articulate critical questions related to services for their child.

○ The parent is part of a team that has in place constructive strategies for managing disagreements.

Parents as Evaluators and Decision Makers at the System Level

Legal Provisions

No Child Left Behind. NCLB requires states and districts to inform parents of their rights to individual decisions they can make for their children relative to school choice, AYP, and highly qualified teachers. NCLB also required states, localities, and Title I schools to report, by special education subgroup, the percentages of students passing statewide tests, graduation rates, and dropout rates. School leaders develop school improvement plans in conjunction with stakeholders, not the least of whom are parents. Schools that engage parents of students with disabilities as evaluators have the potential to implement improvements in overall school performance, special education, and other subgroups.

IDEA provisions. In line with expectations espoused by NCLB, IDEA contains provisions for state and local accountability systems that also focus on results. In addition, IDEA requires state special education departments to report data on 20 key focus areas or "key indicators." Of these key indicators, four are connected to transitioning youth:

> Indicator 1. Percentage of youth with IEPs graduating from high school with a regular diploma compared to percentage of all youth in the State graduating with a regular diploma. (20 U.S.C. § 1416(a)(3)(A))

> Indicator 2. Percentage of youth with IEPs dropping out of high school compared to the percentage of all youth in the State dropping out of high school. (20 U.S.C. § 1416(a)(3)(A))

Indicator 13. Percentage of youth aged 16 and above with an IEP that includes coordinated, measurable, annual IEP goals and transition services that will reasonably enable the student to meet the postsecondary goals. (20 U.S.C. § 1416(a)(3)(B))

Indicator 14. Percentage of youth who had IEPs, are no longer in secondary school and who have been competitively employed, enrolled in some type of postsecondary school, or both, within 1 year of leaving high school. (20 U.S.C. § 1416(a)(3)(B))

These four indicators have transformed the emphasis on preparing students for positive outcomes from a vision to a quantifiable expectation. State and local accountability data for both NCLB and IDEA must be made public. There are sanctions if a locality does not make AYP in performance by all subgroups (including students in special education) for NCLB, and potential sanctions for not meeting acceptable standards for the student population receiving IDEA services.

This heightened accountability for results raises the stakes for practitioners. Parents play a new and more prominent role in program design and evaluation. The previous practice of limiting parental participation to input on the child's IEP, although important, is no longer enough. With an increase in transparency and accountability for student outcomes, parents must assume a new mantle as stakeholder, evaluating how school reform is preparing students to meet the challenges of 21st-century realities. Parents as members of groups who evaluate information can help identify possible issues and solutions.

IDEA requires each state and each local education agency (LEA) to establish a State or Local Advisory Panel with a majority of members as individuals with disabilities or parents of children with disabilities. The state panel advises the state education agency (SEA) on the unmet needs of students with disabilities in the state, and comments publicly on the rules or regulations proposed. In addition, it advises the state on developing evaluative measures and reporting data to the U.S. Office of Special Education Programs. The panel also gives advice to the state on developing corrective action plans to address findings identified in federal monitoring reports and on developing and implementing policies related to coordinating services for students with disabilities. Finally, the State Advisory Panel conducts meetings available to the public and submits an annual report to the state. The Local Advisory Panels perform the same functions within the local districts (20 USC § 1412, Sec. 612(21)(B)).

The inclusion of parent perspectives on these panels is an acknowledgement of the value they bring to the table. States and districts that are committed to using all stakeholders' perspectives to contribute to school improvement and greater achievement of all students will strategically plan how to acclimate and support parents in this role as evaluator and decision maker at the systemic level.

To illustrate, the Virginia Department of Education brought together a stakeholder group to provide input on the Secondary Indicators of their State Performance Plan (i.e., Indicators 1, 2, 13, and 14). According to middle/secondary transition specialist Marianne Moore, "Parents must be at the table. In their roles as evaluators, they can advise us about what the data mean and what we might be able to do to improve student performance and ultimately student outcomes" (personal communication, November 18, 2008). Two parents who also had expertise in transition were part of the stakeholder group that included representatives from LEAs, secondary instruction, vocational rehabilitation, employment, and higher education. The stakeholder group met to evaluate the success of current practices, interpret the meaning of the data, and identify possible opportunities to improve student performance. Recognizing that good and comprehensive planning is a key element to improving graduation rates and postsecondary outcomes, one of the parents suggested developing a model transition plan which would provide a framework to help schools, parents, and students develop the transition components of IEPs. That tool was collaboratively developed and will be available on the Virginia Department of Education Web site.

In addition to IDEA performance indicators for youth with disabilities, states and localities must also report on how parents evaluate their special education services through the deployment of Indicator 8 measures, which measure the "percent of parents with a child receiving special education services who report that schools facilitated parent involvement as a means of improving services and results for children with disabilities" (20 U.S.C. 1416(a)(3)(A)).

For the first time, the federal government required states and localities to gather data about parent satisfaction with their involvement. The National Center for Special Education Accountability and Measurement developed a survey to measure parent satisfaction for Indicator 8 on State Performance Plans and a module entitled *Education Improving Relationships & Results: Building Family School Partnerships* for professionals who wish to improve parental participation (Flammer-Rivera, Giovingo, Paczak, & Coulter, 2008). Special education technical assistance providers funded through the U.S. Department of Education have posted materials identifying where to find additional resources (National Dissemination Center for Children with Disabilities, n.d.). at. States and districts will use the findings from Indicator 8 to evaluate their own effectiveness and improve methods of engaging parents. This topic is discussed more fully in Chapter 8.

Valuable Contributions by Diverse Families

Often overlooked is the importance of parents from diverse cultures having representation as evaluators and decision makers. Parents have had a very strong advocacy voice in educational policy and legislation. However, the parents who have been the most vocal are the ones who are familiar with the system and how it works, and who have the confidence and experience to make sure that their voice is heard. When one looks at the demographics of students in the older grades, it is striking to see the number of students from families living in poverty.

NLTS2 investigated a nationally representative sample of more than 11,000 youth who on December 1, 2000, were ages 13 through 16, receiving special education, and in at least seventh grade. Information was gathered from parents/guardians of NLTS2 youth in telephone interviews or through mail questionnaires in the spring and summer of 2001, 2003, and 2005.

NLTS2 (2007) noted that 36.2% of students resided in households with incomes less than $25,000. Remarkably, 49.3% of students with an intellectual disability and 38.9% of students with an emotional disability came from low-income households. Of all students with disabilities, 35.5% were African American or Hispanic.

The implication of these demographics is that families from diverse cultures have an important voice at the systems evaluation table. Two studies identified in a review of literature by the National Center for Family and Community Connections with Schools (Ferguson, Ramos, Rudo & Wood, 2008) offer examples of the value that diverse voices can bring to evaluative discussions. Cooper (2005) studied Latino families who participated in a 13-week parent institute. In some sites, family members expanded the curriculum of study to areas of need in the community. Families also expressed a desire to participate in decision making and to use their power to influence school reform. This study implied that parent training can lead to more diverse family leadership. Quiocho and Daoud (2006) observed the powerful impact of parents as evaluators in their study of Latino parent involvement. Before a public meeting to discuss the study, the authors heard from teachers that parents were unreliable, refused to volunteer, and that they did not care about their children's education. Counter to this perception, 250 parents came to the meeting in one school and 80 parents came to the meeting at a second school. The authors summarized the themes from the family data:

> The messages from Latino parents were clear. Teach our children the content you teach other students. Expect that our children will achieve, and make sure you support their achievement. Help them, when they need academic help. Make them feel like members of the school community by seeing their faces, understanding their personalities, and valuing their needs. Parents felt that the schools were not offering their children a quality education, and they wanted the schools to be accountable for that. At one school, the teachers and administrators were offended by the candidness of parents and placed Spanish-speaking parents with English-only speaking adults (teachers and other parents) at subsequent meetings. This effectively silenced the voices of additional concerns of Spanish-speaking parents. (Quiocho & Daoud, 2006, p. 264)

Strategies to Support Parents' Assimilation Into Systems-Level Evaluators and Decision Makers

Schools and agencies that recognize the valuable contributions of parents as decision makers and evaluators can help support more active participation of families in this role by establishing a welcoming and secure context. Parents want and need to trust that their perspectives are appreciated and valued. They want to know what will be expected of them as decision makers and evaluators, and they need to feel confident that their views will not jeopardize current levels of service for their children and other families. Using common language that is free from acronyms and industry jargon will help parents understand the discussion and make them be more confident in articulating questions, ideas and concerns. They may want to connect with veteran experienced parents to gain knowledge and a broader perspective, preferably ones who have already served in evaluative roles. Practitioners who want to empower parents in the role of decision maker and evaluator at the systems level will need professional development and support beyond what is available in this book. Rhode Island developed a directory of opportunities for parents to get involved in state policy and planning, with an introductory discussion of the issues and supports parents will need (Rhode Island Kids Count, 2004).

Parents who serve as system evaluators and decision makers will need to expand their knowledge beyond their individual expertise with their own child. Parents who want to influence the effectiveness of program improvement by serving on these panels and policy committees and those who want to make a short-term impact should have certain background knowledge:

1. *Parents need to understand the underlying purposes of transition* and the purpose of the policy group. At the end of the day, how will their participation be a benefit to transition programming for all families?

2. *Parents must have an understanding of schoolwide reform* in the context of real-world expectations for college and career readiness.

3. *Parents need easy-to-understand information about state or district policy* as it relates to transition programming and practices, including student preferences, interests, strengths, needs, and the value of supporting postsecondary goals relating to education, training, employment, and independent living skills, as well as high school diploma options in their state.

4. *Parents need information about disabilities* other than their child's and how these disabilities affect the needs and outcomes of youth during the transition years.

5. *Parents need to understand the value of data collection,* how to interpret data, and how to access the data related to NCLB, IDEA, and other relevant sources.

6. *Parents need to know the socioeconomic and cultural demographic picture of those who live in their communities.* Their participation on local and state committees and commissions will be effective if in conjunction with their personal experiences they can also provide the perspective of other families whose children have different disabilities and are of different socioeconomic backgrounds. All information will need to be available in alternate formats, including multiple language translations as needed for the use of parents on advisory panels and for their dissemination to other parents.

7. *Parents must have a realistic understanding of budgetary restrictions* and an awareness of what adult service provider agencies can and cannot do.

8. *Parents need opportunities to meet with other families* to listen to concerns and to practice communicating about the issues—if they truly are to represent views of experiences beyond their own. As family members join local and state policy committees to evaluate transition program efforts, transition personnel will need to create systems in support of

parents as decision makers and evaluators as they gather critical information sets as indicated earlier. There are some practices already in place, mostly sponsored by federally or state-funded parent information and training centers.

Practitioners can send parents to the Standard & Poor's reader-friendly SchoolMatters Web site (2009) for a quick comparison of schools in their communities to see how students scored in reading and math according to statewide testing, and can direct them to their state departments of education Web sites to learn how students with disabilities within their own districts are performing. They can download special education outcomes in the 20 key indicators for their local schools as well as a state compilation. Additionally, parents can learn how academic achievement and annual yearly progress are being reported locally and statewide for the general education community. These snapshots can help parents form opinions of the importance of data collection and how their children's' schools are doing across multiple fronts. With this additional information parents can more effectively act as evaluators of their school's efforts to support all students in preparation for adult life, drawing more substantive conclusions about transition program design.

For information focused on transition issues, PEATC (2008) developed the Next Steps training, a series of workshops designed to be by a trained teacher, parent, and rehabilitation counselor team. These informative workshops are provided to combined audiences of parents and practitioners in ways that build collaboration between these stakeholders. Several states offer the Next Steps workshops regularly. Parents who attend these workshops develop the knowledge and skills base they would need to effectively function on an advisory group.

States, districts, or agencies may want to develop a guidebook for parents who agree to serve on committees, boards or advisory panels like the one developed by Gerst, Holden, Norwood, and Sykes (2001). Their guide was written for parents who serve on the Interagency Coordinating Council for early childhood programs, but the chapter key questions could just as well be written for an advisory committee considering secondary transition (see box, "Questions for Parent Representatives").

Partners in Policymaking is an internationally embraced program for supporting individuals with disabilities and their families to develop the knowledge and skills they will need to become leaders in evaluation and decision making at the governmental policy level. Founded in 1987 in Minnesota, this program has grown to include classroom trainings, online sessions, and homework assignments. According to their Web site, by 2007, "More than 15,000 Partners graduates are part of a growing national and international network of community leaders serving on policy making committees, commissions, and boards at all levels of government" (Minnesota's Governor's Council on Developmental Disabilities, 2007).

Conclusion

Practitioners and leadership in educational and community transition service agencies in today's accountability climate are continually engaged in

QUESTIONS FOR PARENT REPRESENTATIVES

- What is the position of parent representative all about?
- Who is on the committee?
- What role do the subcommittees play?
- When should I tell my story?
- How can I broaden my base of information and experience?
- What is my constituency?
- How do I know if I've made a difference?

discussion of how to improve their services to ensure stronger outcomes for the youth they serve. Parents are a valuable, often underutilized resource to them. If practitioners build collaborative partnerships with parents in planning and implementing services for individual youths, parents can contribute a "whole-person" perspective in evaluating the effectiveness of services and programs. When parents are encouraged to voice their vision, expectations, and frustrations, team members will see strengths and gaps in services from a new perspective. When parents are included as partners in decision making for their young adults, they often ask questions that reveal new options or variations on current practices that would improve the overall program not only for their own child but for others. School and agency leaders who are truly committed to improving their systems will empower these parents to become more than token members of system-level evaluative and decision-making boards and panels. In the history of disability services in this country and abroad, it has been the vocal parents who have changed the system; in the past, however, they had to go outside the system, using legal and political venues, to make themselves heard. There will always be parents with the drive to improve the system through sharing their informed critique of the status quo and participating in collaborative decision making related specifically to their own child or wholly to current practices. Organizations must include provisions for parents' voices to be heard as evaluators and decision makers as a critical component of ongoing systems improvement.

INDICATORS OF SUCCESS FOR EFFECTIVE SERVICE EVALUATORS AND DECISION MAKERS AT THE SYSTEMS LEVEL

○ Parents function as full members of advisory groups and are comfortable asking questions and contributing information. They have a clear understanding of the goals of the group and the value of their contribution. The group has a fundamental understanding of the parent's role and values his/her participation in the process.

○ Parents have a fundamental understanding of the transition process, program policies, funding, and requirements within school-age programs as well as available adult service systems.

○ Parents access relevant data, know how to interpret it, and contribute to discussions of data implications.

○ Parents offer information about the diverse needs of families in their communities. The group assumes responsibility for learning about the priorities, needs, thoughts, and desires of diverse families—this is not just the parent representative's job.

○ Common language is a normal part of the conversation, and professionals are proactive in providing clarification when using acronyms or industry jargon.

REFERENCES

Center for Education Reform. (2008). *Evaluating your child's school: Questions to ask.* Retrieved November 18, 2008, from http://www.edreform.com/parentPower/101/ accountability.htm

Cooper, C. M. (2005). Evaluating parent empowerment: A look at the potential of social justice evaluation in education. *Teachers College Record, 107,* 2248–2274.

Epstein, J. L. (2005, September). *Developing and sustaining research-based programs of school, family, and community partnerships: Summary of five years of NNPS research.* Retrieved July 7, 2008, from http://www.csos.jhu.edu/P2000/pdf/Research% 20Summary.pdf

Epstein, J. L., Sanders, M. G., & Sheldon, S. B. (2007). *Family and community involvement: Achievement effects.* Retrieved July 7, 2008, from http://www.csos.jhu.edu/ P2000/pdf/NICHD%20Progress%20Report%20Summary%2007.pdf

Ferguson, C., Ramos, M., Rudo, Z., & Wood, L. (2008). *The school–family connection: Looking at the larger picture. A review of current literature.* Austin, TX: National Center for Family and Community Connections with Schools.

Flammer-Rivera, L. M., Giovingo, L., Paczak, H. A., & Coulter, W. A. (2008). *Improving relationships & results: Building family school partnerships.* New Orleans, LA: National Center for Special Education Accountability Monitoring (NCSEAM). Retrieved November 30, 2008, from http://www.accountabilitydata.org/bbfiles/ introduction%20material/cover%20and%20developers.pdf

Gerst, D., Holden, L., Norwood, C., & Sykes, D. (2001). *Go ask Alice: A guidebook for parents serving on state and local interagency councils.* Columbus, OH: The Ohio State University Research Foundation. Retrieved September 25, 2008, from http://www. eric.ed.gov/ERICWebPortal/recordDetail?accno=ED350731

Individuals With Disabilities Education Improvement Act of 2004, 20 U.S.C. §1400 *et seq.* (2004).

Kochhar-Bryant, C., & Greene, G. (2009). *Pathways to successful transition for youth with disabilities: A developmental process* (2nd ed.). Upper Saddle River, NJ: Merrill.

Kreider, H., Caspe, M., Kennedy, S., & Weiss, H. (2007, Spring). *Family involvement in middle and high school students' education* (Family Involvement Makes a Difference, No. 3). Cambridge, MA: Harvard Family Research Project.

Merriam-Webster Online. (2008). Springfield, MA: Merriam-Webster. Retrieved December 26, 2008, from www.merriam-webster.com

Minnesota's Governor's Council on Developmental Disabilities. (2007). *Partners in Policymaking.* St. Paul: Author. Retrieved December 28, 2008, from http://www. partnersinpolicymaking.com/index.html

National Dissemination Center for Children with Disabilities. (n.d.). *Resources: Part B indicators.* Washington, DC: Author. Available http://www.nichcy.org/ InformationResources/Pages/PartBIndicators.aspx

National Longitudinal Transition Study 2. (2007). [Data tables]. Unpublished raw data. Retrieved July 30, 2008, from www.nlts2.org

No Child Left Behind Act of 2001, 20 U.S.C. § 6301 *et seq.* (2002).

Parent Educational Advocacy Training Center. (2008). *NEXT STEPS transition team training.* Falls Church, VA: Author.

Quiocho, A. M. L., & Daoud, A. M. (2006). Dispelling myths about Latino parent participation in schools. *The Educational Forum, 70,* 255–267.

Rhode Island Kids Count. (2004, November). *Parent engagement in state policy and planning; A directory of opportunities for parents to get involved in state policy and planning.* Providence, RI: Author. Retrieved September 25, 2008, from www.rikidscount. org/matriarch/switch.asp_Q_PageID_E_202_A_PageName_E_ohter_A_ LinksPageID_E_683

Roundtable discussion: Meeting the highly qualified teacher criteria for special education teachers. Hearing before the subcommittee on education and early childhood development of the committee on health, education, labor and pensions, United States Senate, 109th Cong. (2005) (testimony of Jeffrey Langham).

Schoeller, K., & Emanuel, E. (2003). Parents as evaluators and decision-makers. In D. L. Wandry & A. M. Pleet (Eds.), *A practitioner's guide to involving families in secondary transition* (pp. 41–58). Reston,VA: Council for Exceptional Children.

Sheldon, S. B., & Epstein, J. L. (2005). School programs of family and community involvement to support children's reading and literacy development across the grades. In J. Flood & P. Anders (Eds.), *Literacy development of students in urban schools: Research and policy.* (pp. 107–138). Newark, DE: International Reading Association.

Standard & Poor's. (2009). *SchoolMatters.* New York: McGraw-Hill. Available http://www.schoolmatters.com/

Wagner, M., Newman, L., Cameto, R., Levine, P., & Garza, N. (2006, August). *An overview of findings from wave 2 of the National Longitudinal Transition Study-2* (NLTS-2). Menlo Park, CA: SRI International.

ABOUT THE AUTHORS

CHERIE TAKEMOTO is Executive Director of the Parent Educational Advocacy Training Center (PEATC), Virginia's parent support, training, and information center committed to building better futures for children with disabilities, their families, and the professionals who serve them. Much of her work has focused on building partnerships to collaboratively address problems families of children with disabilities face. Takemoto served on the President's Commission on Excellence in Special Education, and is currently on a number of national and state advisory boards related to special education. She has struggled to find new ways to address old problems and complaints while fully embracing her charge to improve results for students with disabilities. She is co-author of the 4th edition of *Negotiating the Special Education Maze* (Woodbine House, 2008).

CATHY HEALY is Director of Training and the Project Director of an RSA transition grant at PEATC. As a former Joseph P. Kennedy Public Policy Fellow assigned to the U.S. Department of Labor Office of Disability Employment Policy, she was employed by the U.S. Chamber of Commerce Institute for a Competitive Workforce as a Director of Workforce Programs with a focus on nontraditional populations. She was a founding member of the U.S. Business Leadership Network (USBLN)®, an employer organization committed to advancing the recruiting and hiring of individuals with disabilities. She currently serves on the USBLN® corporate advisory board and is an officer on the Board of Directors with ICON Community Services, continuing the effort to ensure employment opportunities are available to transitioning youth with disabilities.

6

Parents as Peer Mentors

Suzanne Ripley

ESSENTIAL QUESTIONS

○ What are the critical opportunities and challenges for parents to use the support of other parents during the transition process (e.g., assessment, planning, service selection, procedural safeguards, disability information, advocacy)?

○ What supports are available to help parents train and mentor other parents in these opportunities (e.g., parent support centers, national organizations)?

○ What prerequisite skills and knowledge do parents and practitioners need to energize this parental role?

As young adults with disabilities move from school-based services and settings to postschool roles and providers, family members have significant changes in informational needs. Throughout the school years, their children were in relatively predictable settings, and they were operating under similar policies and legally mandated procedural safeguards. In the transitional years, those same youth with disabilities begin to use multiple services, many of which may not be coordinated and may operate under different policies and procedures, using new terminology and dealing with different procedural tasks. Parents discover that simply relying on school personnel to anticipate needs and provide services—which worked in the past—is insufficient. At the same time, there may be a shift from family members celebrating growth and accomplishments to focusing on descriptions of those same youths' deficits as eligibility is sought for services that may have puzzling, frustrating priorities and wait lists. Initially, parents may feel isolated, not knowing where to begin their search for information, assistance, understanding, and support (Smith, 1997).

During this confusing change in services and terminology, parents learn that other parents and their sons and daughters are experiencing it simultaneously, and many have done so already. The purpose of this chapter is to explore the roles of parents supporting other parents through the transition process as peer mentors.

101

Defining "Peer Mentors"

Mentoring is defined as a nurturing process, wherein a more experienced or skilled person functions as a role model, and engages in teaching, encouraging, sponsoring, and counseling a less experienced or less skilled person, with the intent of promoting the latter's professional or personal development (Lock et al., 2006). The mentor has moved beyond the traditional role of information recipient into the more proactive role of assisting others to gain and use that same information. Further, *peer support* functions as a system of giving and receiving assistance based on respect, shared responsibility, and mutual understanding of what is helpful to self and others. Mentors relate to another's situation through shared experiences and relationships that promote growth and wellness.

Benefits of Parents as Peer Mentors

Benefits to Parents and Practitioners

Layzer, Goodson, Bernstein, and Price's study of parent support programs (2001) found that effective support programs involve peer-mentoring components. Research on organized parent mentor practices report benefits for both parents and practitioners. Involvement in these practices increases positive parental attitude and knowledge to a greater degree than those without peer support (Cohen & Canan, 2006). According to Cohen and Canan, "the role of the parent [mentor] is to provide families with information, support, and guidance as they negotiate the system so they can have successful interactions with the system" (p. 868). Parents who become resources not only assist others, but also benefit as well, continually improving their own systemic knowledge.

Santelli (2002), referring to formal Parent-to-Parent programs, cited benefits to involved families as (a) providing opportunities to talk about the impact of disability on the family structure; (b) allowing parents to discuss the stress of dealing with multiple providers, learning new vocabulary, and addressing possible financial implications; (c) helping parents find support and advice about services; (d) assisting parents in sustaining healthy family infrastructure, given added stressors related to disability; and (e) helping parents learn how to have confidence in their own ideas for their children. Although the Parent-to-Parent model is not exclusive to transition-age supports, the implications are clear that the need for support is ongoing, and although the providers and the settings may change, the stressors continue and the need for support most likely does not abate. In addition, these types of supports—both informational and emotional—may be very different from supports professionals offer (Santelli). When parents function as mentors to other parents, (a) linkages are developed, (b) recommendations to other parents from other perspectives are shared, and (c) parents receive specific, focused knowledge of service protocol, contact persons, and strategies for moving successfully through respective systems (Matthews & Hudson, 2001). Therefore, parents benefit by developing a support and training network of individuals with similar concerns, and school and agency practitioners benefit from the shared ownership and responsibility, as well as their exposure to the knowledge, perspective, and assistance from parents (Kolb, 2003).

> ❝ I've encountered scared parents of young adults with disabilities who are seeking answers and supports for themselves as well as for their youth as they enter transitional age. They ask, "Where does a mother or father go to talk with peers who are having similar experiences? Where can parents find someone who has been through this with their young adult and worked it all out? We had people to talk to during the school years but where are they all now? Did they do everything perfectly and now their sons and daughters are independent, successful and happy? Am I the only one who is losing sleep here?" ❞
>
> *Suzanne Ripley*

Benefits to Students

The overall benefit to students of parents who are actively engaged in their educational process is well documented. Parents serve as role models for their children, and continue in that role through the transition planning process (Landmark, Zhang, & Montoya, 2007; Lee & Wehmeyer, 2004). Positive relationships with professionals and ongoing involvement in promoting positive educational outcomes for their children enhances the potential for better school attendance; reduced dropout rates; higher assessment scores; and improved student attitude, self-confidence, and social competence (Landmark et al.; Patrikakou, 2004; Whitbread, Bruder, Fleming, & Park, 2007). Parent-involved character education has been found to increase student performance and decrease unwanted behaviors (Martin & Martin, 2007). According to Henderson and Mapp (2005), these findings regarding positive effects of parental involvement tend to hold true across races, ethnicities, income levels, and educational backgrounds.

Parents of transition-age youth who want to continue beneficial involvement with practitioners may have difficulties doing so, as their priorities shift in response to the emerging independence of their youth. It is natural for parents of young adults with disabilities to have concerns as their sons and daughters enter new environments. Although successful movement to postschool roles is a source of pride, parents of any child don't stop worrying anywhere along the transition process to adulthood. They worry about their youths getting along with co-workers, being included in social activities, and making friends. Or, when they are included, parents can worry about that, too. They worry about public transportation, as well as the alarming statistics about youthful drivers. These concerns may be magnified for parents of youth with disabilities, who, during this time of emotional fragility, may have new and unfamiliar support needs. However, as their young adults get more opportunities in the local community, in regular work sites and recreation programs, there actually may be even less opportunity for parents to connect with other parents who are their peers. If families can connect to well-informed, experienced peers who can guide them through these transitional concerns, there will be increased opportunities for their sons and daughters with disabilities to access full citizenship.

Parents who engage in peer support as a context for positive decision making can recognize and use available supports and opportunities to change their own behaviors and appropriately react to problems. Young adults with disabilities, along with their families, benefit from encouragement on all fronts to create a vision of adulthood, and receive opportunities to share their dreams, fears, and frustrations in a rich dialog. If families can build well-informed "safety nets" amid the fear of risk taking that are part of the young adult experience, autonomy, independence, and constructive role-related changes will increase for that young adult (Petersen, 2004). When families have the opportunity to connect with experienced peers who can guide them through these transitional concerns, they gain additional information and the confidence they need to let their sons and daughters experience independence and make decisions for themselves.

The nature of the disability is a consideration in engendering risk taking, as well as student ownership. For a young person with cognitive, emotional, and/or psychiatric disabilities, decision making may be limited; this young person may continue to need the support and assistance of parents and family to make independent decisions and implement plans. Person-centered planning requires participation of the person with the disability to the greatest extent possible. In some instances, person-centered planning may not involve the parents at all. This is especially true once the age of majority has been reached. At that time, per the mandates of the Individuals With Disabilities Education Improvement Act of 2004 (IDEA), states may elect to transfer educational decision-making rights to students who are "competent to give informed consent in decisions" at the age of majority, giving them the right to make informed decisions and be responsible for their own educational program (National Center on Secondary Education and Transition, 2002).

This growing autonomy of youth can be difficult for parents who may benefit peer support to address their discomfort and fears. Gathering this support will assist the parents in phasing out supervisory roles for their young adults, thus increasing the potential for their youths' self-determination and ownership of the transition process to the maximum extent possible. It is important to remember that parent mentor models exist in formal, researched, and developed forms, as well as in situational, informal, individualized forms—both of which are discussed later in the chapter.

    ❝ Challenges include trying to change the perceptions and belief systems of the parents. They often confuse empowering the young adults with abandoning their parental responsibilities. ❞

        Sergio Fernandez, Vocational Rehabilitation District Representative, AZ

Considerations in Supporting Parents in Peer Mentor Roles

Kolb (2003) identified several possible challenges to practitioners supporting parents and families in these emergent roles: (a) personal view, (b) parent and professional perceptions, and (c) availability.

Personal View

Parents tend to view disability and transition issues solely from the perspective of their child, thus limiting the value of the parent's contribution to the whole group (Guy, Goldberg, McDonald, & Flom, 1997). They may only have information about their own child's disability and the challenges they have faced. They need a broader base of information about the range of disabilities and transition planning procedures and outcomes before they will be able to support other parents whose children may have different disabilities.

As they move beyond a personal view into a more global view, parents need to identify the systems context of transition and, as mentors, provide other parents assistance with processes rather than specific services. These include the process for planning transition, the processes governing the school's curricular responsibilities during transition, and exploration of options in adult life. Processes include discussion of person-centered planning and mapping. The services should be individualized; the process for accessing services is more generic and global. Of course, mentors can still share more general information as applied to the individual needs of the student. For example, Mrs. Rodriguez can help Mrs. Jones understand the different service options and eligibility criteria for community work experiences, beyond what her own son is receiving. She also can mentor Mrs. Rodriguez in accessing those services on behalf of her own child.

Parent and Professional Perceptions

Practitioners need to examine their own perceptions about the value of parent contributions in this role. If they believe that parents' contributions are somehow of less value than their own expert contributions, they will have difficulty empowering parents to assume this role. Parents also may have perceptions that could interfere with their ability to function in this role. Friesen and Huff (1990) identified parental concerns of cooptation, that is, their concerns of being dominated as they are assimilated into the educational system. Friesen and Huff explained how a parent's involvement in a system that may have attempted to minimize the advocacy effort of that individual is a conflict of interest for both the parent and the professional. One example of cooptation is when a parent who serves as a school-sponsored mentor feels reluctant to express his or her feelings because they may be perceived as challenging the expertise of the professional and potentially cause conflict in future professional interactions. Parents may have the perspective that the transition process provides one silo for practitioners, another for them, and another for their youth, rather than a potentially collegial process, An awareness of possible conflicts between parent and professional perceptions will lead to an open discussion of the issues and can make an important contribution to building partnerships between parents and practitioners. Parent support networks can provide guidance for families new to postschool systems, as parent roles shift from making choices for their young adults to supporting their children's self-advocacy and relationships with service practitioners.

Availability

Availability concerns about the development of parents as mentors include both availability of parents and availability of support from professionals. Friesen and Huff (1990) identified certain factors including the lack of parents' ability to fulfill the numerous demands these roles placed upon them, such as time and financial constraints, and parental involvement in other roles as challenges in this process. These concerns also include difficulties in contacting parents, scheduling conflicts, and parent withdrawal from involvement when they do not feel validated by school and agency practitioners (Guy et al., 1997). Friesen and Huff also commented on the high expectations that some professionals place on parents, such as presuming that parents can readjust their work and home schedules to attend meetings scheduled at times convenient for educators, or arranging child care in order to attend meetings. Time issues, for both parents and professionals, must be addressed. Finally, the availability of funding to support parent training is another significant barrier to assisting parents in their role as peer mentors.

Resolving these issues requires careful communication in identifying the positions and perspectives of each individual. Parents need to understand the legal and systematic constraints that professionals must operate within to support their agencies, and how those procedures may create barriers to service availability. Professionals and parents need to discuss these constraints to maintain positive relations with all stakeholders. Otherwise, collaborative effort may be jeopardized and/or parents' anger and frustration with the legal system or inadequate resources may be inappropriately directed at the same professional who provided the mentoring and support (Friesen & Huff, 1990).

Mentor Networks and Models

Formal Mentorship Models

Parent mentorship networks have been established in many locations to provide support to parents for specific purposes. In a national study of parent assistance models particular to alternative dispute resolution, Henderson (2008) found that 26 of the 43 respondent states indicated parent assistance was a component of the resolution process; this was defined as parents serving as resources to other parents and school district personnel for addressing emerging or active conflicts. However, there was significant variability in the nature of that assistance; some states reported assistance coming from formal parent support groups such as state Parent Training Information Centers, whereas others reported a parent-to-parent approach. Henderson also found that some states employ a state education agency-level staff person who, as a parent of a child with a disability, serves as an initial contact and information clearinghouse. Some states, such as Virginia, employ parent ombudsmen at the district level, whereas Oregon actively trains parents to serve as mentors during individualized education program (IEP) meetings. Whatever the approach, a consistent pattern is that effective mentor networks provide opportunities to serve parents both individually and collectively.

Parent-to-parent models. A widely regarded approach to parent mentorships is the parent-to-parent model, which exemplifies the very definition of mentorship cited earlier in this chapter: a more experienced or skilled person functioning as a role model, and engaging in teaching, encouraging, sponsoring, and counseling a less experienced or less skilled person, with the intent of promoting the latter's professional or personal development (Lock et al., 2006). This model is seen as an effective way to build the capacity of social support systems for parents.

Train the trainer. Another suggested approach to building parental capacity in mentor roles is the train-the-trainer model, wherein established parent advocacy agencies facilitate the joint training of parents and professionals in transition-specific topics (e.g., person-centered planning, legal processes and procedures, components of effective school-agency-family partnerships; Whitbread et al., 2007). By engaging in a collaborative learning process, participants are able not only to have a clearer insight into the perspectives of their counterparts, but also to experience a training methodology that can be replicated individually and collaboratively at local levels.

Informal Mentorship Approaches

Due to the growth and increasingly easy use of electronic venues (e.g., social-networking Web sites, blogs, and wikis), individuals can meet and talk via various types of online discussions. Parents and family members can ask questions, get suggestions, and make decisions based on input of others they have never met personally but who seem to share their interests and concerns.

Informal mentoring, like more formal models, still takes place between peers; in this case, they are peers who are addressing the upcoming or recently completed transition from high school to further education, employment, and community living. It is both a sharing of facts and resources and providing emotional support. Parents who are in the process of letting go of control and direction of their sons and daughters may experience a great deal of anxiety combined with pride and hopefulness. Parents of young adults with disabilities experience additional anxiety as they worry about safety and "good" decisions. Their children may be more vulnerable than others due to limitations caused by the disability. Sometimes an informal interaction is more spontaneous and can address immediate areas of concern or crises.

❝ We had informal support groups—getting together around an issue and helping one another examine possibilities and share which programs address those issues and needs and which do not. ❞

Diane H., Parent, MN

Knowledge and Skills Needed to Fulfill Peer Mentor Roles

As parents move into this emergent role of support to other parents, particular knowledge and skill sets are critical, and should be the focus for self-directed information seeking, as well as information provided by practitioners:

- *Information about their own child's disability and the impact on his or her functioning, curriculum, and outcomes, as well as other disabilities represented in families in their network.*

- *Information about parental acceptance stages in adjusting to having a child with a disability.* Parents needing support will be at different junctures in the acceptance process. For example, a family whose child was diagnosed at a young age with a learning disability may have hoped in vain that school would ameliorate that disability by graduation. Another family of a young adult with developmental disabilities diagnosed at birth may have long ago accepted the implications of that child's life-long disability. Finally, a third family may be adjusting to a teenager with a recently acquired traumatic brain injury from a car accident. Even though all three parents have young adults entering the transition phase, they likely will be at very different stages of acceptance. Because of this variability among parents needing support and information, mentors must be fully versed in theories about psychological stages of acceptance and learn not to project their own adjustment progress on families who may not be adjusting as well or as quickly as they may have.

- *Cultural diversity of the community and awareness of differences in values and communication styles.* Parents from diverse cultures face additional challenges and barriers when attempting to become involved in their young adult's transition from school to adulthood, including limited minority leadership representation in schools, lack of knowledge about special education and transition, parental anxiety born of prior unsatisfying relationships with schools, and language barriers (Landmark et al., 2007). Mentors should be representative of various ethnic, racial, economic, and geographic groups and be matched accordingly with the families they are supporting. The common bond of parenting is strong, but not all parents have the same life experiences or expectations, so a cultural match is important. When this isn't possible, sensitivity is critical.

- *Agility in tailoring responsiveness to parent needs.* Skills sets possessed and demonstrated by effective mentors can be identified and applied from other systems. Lock and colleagues (2006) identified several desired skills sets among school professionals serving as mentors to their colleagues, which can be translated to applications relevant to parents serving as mentors to other parents. These skills include:

  1. *Building an expanding network of support by identifying contacts for help or ongoing assistance.* For teachers, this means awareness of whom to contact for emergencies, materials and supplies, technology support, and the like. For parent mentors, this could mean awareness of contacts for IEP meeting support, accurate information on avail-

able community resources on an as-needed basis, or emotional support.

2. *Sharing knowledge and information by reaching out to mentees in non-threatening ways that invite both giving and sharing.* For teachers, this might mean an exchange of ideas regarding the use of technology, while openly admitting that neither the mentor nor the mentee has exclusive expertise in the topic. Similarly, parents who are mentoring or training other parents (e.g., in effective ways to be proactive in IEP transition planning) should be open to shared experiences that may in turn broaden their own repertoire of information; such an interchange not only assists the mentee parents, but also other parents the mentor parent may encounter in the future.

3. *Considering the most desired way to be treated.* This gives an opportunity for a mentor to engage in self-examination as to how value-laden discussions are handled, sensitive concerns are addressed, and information is packaged. Although teachers may benefit from constructive feedback about lesson planning, a parent of a transitioning student with a disability will be more accepting of mentoring and guidance offered in a nonjudgmental, productive manner. Lock et al. (2006) suggest that mentors consider how they would want to be treated when receiving feedback or guidance from others (e.g., teachers, administrators, etc.), and employ those same principles when interacting with their mentees. This is an especially relevant stance when one considers the prevalence of parents who feel that they are not valued or listened to during IEP transition planning (Landmark et al., 2007).

4. *Striking a balance.* Inherent in a mentorship relationship is the perceived authority status of the mentor. This requires that the mentor not abuse that perception, but rather strike a balance between being one who gives information and one who empowers the recipient. The mentor is in an advisory role in this relationship, not an authoritative one. Mentors must be able to rely on their own knowledge and confidence, yet be flexible with new ideas and innovative thinking from the mentee parents as the latter become more confident in their own knowledge and abilities. This might mean providing them with contacts for appropriate community transition agency supports; encouraging them to make those contacts and gather needed information; and then evaluate their preferences in concert with their youth as informed decision makers. In addition, parents may need an explanation of the system and the process as well as strategies for negotiating that system to accomplish their individual goals. Helping mentee families learn what to do if calls are not returned, meetings are cancelled, waiting lists are long, and staff shortages abound addresses the realities of the system and sets the stage for the mentees to become more confident in procedural matters.

5. *Understanding legislative mandates and procedures related to transition.* In particular, since the passage of IDEA in 1997, procedures and implications related to the age of majority have frequently been the

source of family confusion and concerns. Further, because the age of onset for transition planning shifts with each IDEA reauthorization, parents need guidance and support in proactively seeking timely IEP transition planning. Parents who are trained to serve as mentors to other parents during IEP, transition, or mediation meetings can help them prepare for the meeting, clarify roles, plan an agenda, and identify the issues. At the meetings, mentors might take notes and act as informed listeners familiar with special education rules and regulations (Henderson, 2008). In addition, mentors can assist their mentee parents in becoming familiar with the palette of laws other than IDEA that also affect transition during the school and into the adult years. IDEA jurisdiction expires at graduation or age 21, so partner laws governing lifespan access and supports such as the Americans With Disabilities Act of 1990, the Rehabilitation Act of 1973, the Developmental Disabilities Act of 1984 (later the Developmental Disabilities Assistance and Bill of Rights Act), and the Workforce Investment Act of 1998 are critical to the creation of ongoing service linkages. During curricula and career planning, the student and family need to learn about policies governing adult opportunities and bring that information into transition planning discussions.

- *Identification of local program and community resources and services, including availability, eligibility requirements, service options, application procedures and policies.* The National Dissemination Center for Children With Disabilities receives frequent queries from parents about funding/scholarships and assistance on campus for young adults planning on postsecondary education, and adult employment systems (including job development, placement, and support) and transportation for those young adults who are entering the workforce. In addition, frequently sought information focuses on housing options, financial assistance, eligibility for Social Security benefits or ongoing insurance coverage, including adult medical and dental care when their son/daughter is no longer eligible for pediatric health care (see box, "Informational Web Sites").

Methods to Engage Parents as Peer Mentors

Kolb (2003) suggested two approaches to preparing and supporting parents in peer mentor roles: formal and informal venues. Formal venues and procedures have links to service delivery systems and may include budget, materials, and measurability, whereas informal methods are centered on more spontaneous parent-driven activities. Examples of venues include, as described earlier, parent-to-parent models, as well as formalized training and informal networking.

Parent-to-Parent Models

When determining the information to share with parents and strategies for disseminating this information, it is critical to evaluate the specific parent

INFORMATIONAL WEB SITES

- **ACT—Information for Life's Transitions:** www.act.org/
  ACT is an independent, nonprofit organization that provides educational and career services to students, parents, and professionals in schools, businesses, and government agencies.

- **Employment & Training Administration (ETA):** http://wdr.doleta.gov/research/
  The labor and training agencies of the U.S. Government provide this Web site for public access to abstracts and full reports generated through employment and Training Administration. These publications focus on building the capacity of the workforce investment system to prepare the workforce for the 21st century.

- **Family & Advocates Partnership for Education (FAPE):** http://www.fape.org
  FAPE is a project that aims to inform and educate families and advocates about IDEA.

- **Federal Resources for Educational Excellence (FREE):** http://www.ed.gov/free
  FREE provides numerous resources supported by agencies across the U.S. Federal government. Vocational education is included in the resource list.

- **Fundsnet Online Services Home Site:** www.fundsnetservices.com/
  Fundsnet is a directory of a wide variety of grants, scholarships and financial aid resources.

- **National Center on Secondary Education and Transition (NCSET):** http://www.ncset.org/
  NCSET's goal is to improve secondary education and transition outcomes for families of youth with disabilities by coordinating efforts of national, state and local agencies.

- **National Coalition for Parent Involvement in Education (NCPIE):** www.ncpie.org/
  NCPIE is dedicated to establishing effective family, school, and community partnerships.

- **National Parent Information Network (NPIN):** http://npin.org/
  NPIN is a research-based network that provides information about the process of parenting, and family involvement in education.

- **National Secondary Training and Technical Assistance Center (NSTTAC):** www.nsttac.org
  NSTTAC provides links relevant to transitioning youth and their families.

- **Parent Advocacy Coalition for Educational Rights (PACER Center):** http://www.pacer.org
  PACER is a parents-helping-parents model located in Minnesota that provides assistance to families and materials for parents and professionals across the nation.

- **Parent Educational Advocacy Training Center (PEATC):** http://www.peatc.org/
  PEATC offers training opportunities for parents and professionals who are interested in developing courses for families. A training series called NEXT STEP focuses on skills and information needed for assisting student in achieving transition goals.

- **Support and Training for Exceptional Parents (STEP):** http://www.tnstep.org/
  STEP is a statewide family-to-family program in Tennessee, providing advocacy training, information and support services to parents of children with disabilities.

audience and gather input from parents to effectively share the information parents want and need to know. The first step, therefore, is to collect information regarding interest and support from the community. Practitioner strategies for gathering pertinent information can be accomplished by (a) connecting with a few established stakeholders (parents, administration, agency personnel, community members, teachers); (b) creating a parent survey ascertaining areas of interest, expertise, or desire to meet with other individuals; (c) determining whether there is parental interest in meeting together; and (d) identifying parent backgrounds, skills, talents, and areas of needed support. After collecting this initial data, the group can convene and begin to brainstorm strategies that group members are willing to support and implement. In this planning stage, the role of parents as trainers becomes a critical component in ensuring program success (Kolb, 2003).

Admittedly, the dynamics of establishing such a model are challenging, as parents of young adults with disabilities may already be experiencing frustration, fatigue, or even anger over their experiences as they embark on the transitional phase (Brotherson & Berdine, 1993). Despite these challenges, however, it is beneficial to parents entering the process to engage in a focused interaction with others who can share experienced and informed support. Just as an effective transition program begins with a student-centered planning process aimed at fostering students' self-determination (Test, 2000), an effective parent support effort should seek a parallel sense of parental self-determination.

Formalized Training

Accessing formalized training can expand the skills of parents who are assuming the roles of training and mentoring other parents. Formalized training can provide a solid knowledge base for parents who have a desire to serve in these roles but require specific information and training to develop new skills and enhance current skills (Guy et al., 1997).

Practitioners need to be aware of the resources at the community, state, and federal levels so that they can share information about availability and accessibility of training venues and resources. IDEA provided for each state to have at least one federally funded Parent Training and Information Center that is charged with "assisting parents in understanding the special needs of their child; providing parents with information about child development; and helping parents to acquire the necessary skills that will allow them to support the implementation of their child's IEP or IFSP" (34 C.F.R. 300.34(c)(8)). The PACER Center in Minnesota (www.pacer.org) provides coordination, training, and technical assistance to and through these federally funded parent centers.

Some of the national parent information and training centers have developed collaborative training materials like those published by the Parent Educational Advocacy Training Center (PEATC) in Virginia. PEATC offers a transition series for training parent and professional teams called NEXT STEPS. A trained team comprising a parent, an educator, an adult service provider, and a self-advocate presents workshops (see box, "NEXT STEPS Workshop Topics"). The training materials in this program include a trainer's guide with instructions for activities, flow charts and overhead

NEXT STEPS WORKSHOP TOPICS

- **Transition:** Making It in the Real World
- **Transition Plans:** Roadmaps to The Future
- **Self-Advocacy and Supports:** Keys to Independence
- **Moving On:** Life in the Community
- **Getting Ready:** Preparing for Work While in School
- **Planning Ahead:** Future Finances and Support
- **Adult Life:** Effective Partnerships
- **Adult Life:** Accessing Services

(PEATC, 2008)

materials, and materials for participants. See box, "Informational Web Sites," for an annotated list of additional sources valuable for practitioners and parents who want more information about resources and training models; see also box, "Rehabilitation Services Administration Parent Training Projects."

Informal Parent-Driven Activities

Because of the diverse experience levels of parents, they bring a valuable perspective to other families with children with disabilities. Parents can have significant impact on other families as role models, providing support by modeling effective techniques in meeting the needs of all members of the family. Following are strategies implemented by parents working with other parents with practitioner support. Practitioners should be aware of the multiple benefits of peer parent mentoring, training, and role modeling, and collaborate with parents desiring this level of leadership in finding venues for peer experiences in school, agency, and community settings.

Special education parent support groups. Parents and special education practitioners collaboratively lead monthly meetings, discuss relevant topics, and provide training in advocacy areas. The purpose of this group is to connect parents with educators and parents with other parents in providing a general knowledge base of transition topics and other related services.

"Meet the teacher" and classroom meetings. Parents can meet with other parents of students in the classroom, as well as their children's teachers. These meetings can create an informal opportunity for families to network with other families. Classroom teachers have an opportunity to meet all parents, discuss the curriculum goals, and share information about transition planning before the school year starts. Often there are waiting lists for receiving services from agencies as well as the extensive response time in

REHABILITATION SERVICES ADMINISTRATION PARENT TRAINING PROJECTS

Exceptional Parents Unlimited
4440 North First Street
Fresno, CA 93726
559-229-2000 (Voice)
559-229-2956 FAX
bcoulbourne@exceptionalparents.org
www.exceptionalparents.org

**Family Network On Disabilities
Of Florida**
2735 Whitney Road
Clearwater, FL 33760-1610
727-523-1130 (Voice)
727-523-8687 FAX
fnd@fndfl.org
www.fndfl.org

**Family Resource Center On
Disability**
20 East Jackson Blvd.
Room 300
Chicago, IL 60604
312-939-3513 (Voice)
312-939-7297 FAX
1-800-952-4199 IL only
frcdptiil@ameritech.net
www.frcd.org

Maine Parent Federation
P.O. Box 2067
Augusta, ME 04338-2067
207-623-2144 (Voice)
207-623-2148 FAX
1-800-870-7746
parentconnect@mpf.org
www.mpf.org

Missouri Parents Act (MPACT)
8301 State Line Road, Suite 204
Kansas City, MO 64114
816-531-7070 (Voice)
816-931-2992 (TDD)
816-531-4777 FAX
msavage@ptimpact.org
www.ptimpact.com

PACER Center
8161 Normandale Blvd.
Minneapolis, MN 55437
952-838-9000 (Voice)
952-838-0199 FAX
1-800-537-2237 in MN
pacer@pacer.org
www.pacer.org

**Parent Educational Advocacy
Training Center**
100 North Washington Street
Suite 234
Falls Church, VA 22046
703-923-0010 Voice & TTY
703-923-0030 FAX
1-800-869-6782 in VA
partners@peatc.org
www.peatc.org

processing various forms. Parents can learn which paperwork to file and when to begin certain tasks.

Transition seminars. Practitioners, in collaboration with parent trainers, provide support and training to other parents about transition topics such as school-to-work programs; supported employment; work and life skills; job development, matching, and supervision; functional assessment; and futures planning. These seminars help parents by providing contacts, developing timelines, and gathering or presenting information on support agencies. Appropriate locations for this would be at a local community center or high school.

Parent match or parents paired with parents. Parents and educators organize parent mentor connections matching parents who are experienced in certain areas with parents who are about to go through a similar experience or need support.

Parent-to-parent transition section in the school newsletter. A section of the newsletter prepared by school for all families in the community newsletter, developed in collaboration with educators and parents, is devoted to addressing parents concerns related to areas of transition. Because of the communitywide distribution of the newsletter, numerous community members and agencies have access to the information presented in the newsletter.

Personal and professional contacts. Parents who have personal and professional access to persons with expertise in medical, health, financial, insurance, legal, and advocacy areas could assist in facilitating opportunities for these individuals to share their expertise with other parents. Venues for these resources are transition seminars, PTA meetings, and parent-to-parent meetings.

Parent presentations to organizations. Parents present information about their children's disabilities to parent and service organizations to help create a level of understanding about different disabilities. This establishes community contacts and links parents to potential resources.

Parent social nights provide opportunities for parents to socialize and network with other parents in a more relaxed atmosphere. Parents can informally exchange ideas and strategies that have been effective for facilitating transition services for their children.

Reading club. Parents form reading groups exploring current literature in the field of special education and discuss transition relevant topics.

Email discussion groups, Web sites, blogs, and e-newsletters/parent newsletters. Parents develop a newsletter that can be submitted online to other parents. Parents generate and contribute to the topics and information listed in these Internet mentoring tools. Topics that are identified as valuable resources are defining clear transition goals in the IEP, training seminars that are beneficial for parents, and strategies for increasing student and family involvement in futures planning.

> ❝ We encourage and help parents to become mentors. By doing this, they can empower themselves to become role models. They can support other parents in doing the same, resulting in a network of role models and mentors. ❞
>
> *William J. Schmidt, Director of Day Program Services, AZ*

Conclusion

Parents and professionals acknowledge the importance and value of parents networking with other parents. These networks can provide an avenue of sharing information, expertise, and resources that can be of mutual benefit to families in meeting the transition outcomes for their children. This chapter was designed to provide insights that can help in the facilitation of parents as peer mentors as a starting point in generating new strategies. The possibilities are limitless due to the varied contributions of parents, other family members, practitioners, and other stakeholders. Parents can make unique contributions to other parents because of the shared emotional, knowledge, and skill needs during their youths' transition.

INDICATORS OF SUCCESS FOR EFFECTIVE PEER MENTORING PRACTICES

○ Practitioners have an increased awareness of the benefits and purpose of parents as mentors and frequently refer parents to other parents.

○ Parent mentors are identified as valid resources by other parents and practitioners.

○ Parents report the services and information they receive from other parents are valuable.

○ Parents who have been mentored are prepared to collaborate with school and agency practitioners as partners.

○ Parents are empowered to mentor other parents as their children evolve in the ownership in the transition process.

REFERENCES

Brotherson, M. J., & Berdine, W. R. (1993). Transition to adult services: Support for ongoing parent participation. *Remedial and Special Education, 14*(4), 44–51.

Cohen, E., & Canan, L. (2006). Closer to home: Parent mentors in child welfare. *Child Welfare, 85,* 867–884.

Friesen, B. J., & Huff, B. (1990). Parents and professionals as advocacy partners. *Preventing School Failure, 34*(3), 31–37.

Guy, B., Goldberg, M., McDonald, S., & Flom, R.A. (1997). Parental participation in transition systems change. *Career Development for Exceptional Individuals, 20,* 165–177.

Henderson, A. T., & Mapp, K. L. (2005). *A new wave of evidence: The impact of school, family, and community connections on student achievement. Annual Synthesis.* Austin, TX: National Center for Family and Community Connections with Schools. (ERIC Document Reproduction Service No. ED 47451)

Henderson, K. (2008). *Optional IDEA alternate dispute resolution.* Alexandria, VA: Project Forum, National Association of State Directors of Special Education and Consortium for Appropriate Dispute Resolution in Special Education. Retrieved December 15, 2008 , from http://www.projectforum.org

IDEA Regulations, 71 Fed. Reg. 46540 *et seq.* (August 14, 2006).

Individuals With Disabilities Education Improvement Act of 2004, 20 U.S.C. § 1400 *et seq.* (2004).

Kolb, S. (2003). Parents as trainers, role models, and mentors. In D. L. Wandry & A. M. Pleet (Eds.), *A practitioner's guide to involving families in secondary transition.* Arlington, VA: Council for Exceptional Children.

Landmark, L., Zhang, D., & Montoya, L. (2007). Culturally diverse parents' experiences with their children's transition: Knowledge and involvement. *Career Development for Exceptional Individuals, 30,* 68–79.

Layzer, J. L., Goodson, B. D., Bernstein, L., & Price, C. (2001). *National evaluation of family support programs, final report, volume A: The meta-analysis.* Cambridge, MA: ABT Associates.

Lee, S. H., & Wehmeyer, M. L. (2004). A review of the Korean literature related to self-determination: Future directions and practices in promoting the self-determination of students with disabilities. *Korean Journal of Special Education, 38,* 369–390.

Lock, R. H., Lee, S., Theoharis, M. F., Kim, K., Liss, J. M., Nix-Williams, T., et al. (2006). Create effective mentoring relationships: Strategies for mentor and mentee success. *Intervention in School and Clinic, 41,* 233–240.

Martin, D., & Martin, M. (2007). Implementing a family/school partnership in an urban elementary school to reduce negative behavior and increase academic achievement. *Family Therapy, 34*(3), 141–152.

Matthews, J. M., & Hudson, A. M. (2001). Guidelines for evaluating parent training programs. *Family Relations, 50*(1), 77–87.

National Center on Secondary Education and Transition. (2002). *Age of majority: Preparing your child for making good choices.* Minneapolis, MN: Author.

Parent Education and Training Center. (2008). *NEXT STEPS: Transitioning to adult life.* Falls Church, VA: Author.

Patrikakou, E. N. (2004). *Adolescence: Are parents relevant to students' high school achievement and post-secondary attainment?* Cambridge, MA: Harvard Family Research Project.

Petersen, K. (2004, March). *Supporting the dynamic development of youth with disabilities during transition: A guide for families* (Information Brief Vol. 3 Issue 2: Addressing Trends and Development in Secondary Education and Transition). Minneapolis, MN: National Center on Secondary Education and Transition.

Santelli, B. (2002). *Basics for parents: Parent to parent support.* Washington, DC: National Information Center for Children and Youth with Disabilities.

Smith, P. M. (1997). *You are not alone: For parents when they learn their child has a disability.* Washington, DC: National Information Center for Children and Youth with Disabilities.

Test, D. W. (2000). Implementing the transition mandate: The relationship between programs, personnel, and services. *Special Services in the Schools, 16*(1/2), 23–36.

Whitbread, K. M., Bruder, M. B., Fleming, G., & Park, H. (2007). Collaboration in special education parent professional training. *TEACHING Exceptional Children 39*(4), 6–14.

ABOUT THE AUTHOR

SUZANNE RIPLEY is the Director of the National Dissemination Center for Children With Disabilities at the Academy for Educational Development in Washington, DC. For more than 20 years, she has advised families and educators across the country on how best to serve children with special needs. She also has two sons with multiple disabilities who have received special education services.

7

Parents as Systems Change Agents

Mary E. Morningstar

ESSENTIAL QUESTIONS

○ What are the critical opportunities and challenges for parents to influence systems change during the transition process?

○ What supports are available to help parents acclimate to this role?

○ What are the prerequisite skills and knowledge that parents and practitioners need to energize this parental role?

Some of the most significant changes impacting the lives of individuals with disabilities began with parents and family members taking the role of systems change agents. Historically, parents and family members have been instrumental in major shifts in policies as well as society's views about the inclusion of individuals with disabilities. The "first wave" of parent activism took place in the 1950s with parents forming such key disability organizations as the National Association of Retarded Children (now called The Arc), the United Cerebral Palsy Association, and the Muscular Dystrophy Association (Powers, 1996, p. 415). During these early days, the primary role of parent organizations was to keep children with disabilities from harm especially in institutional settings, to support research, to raise money, and to advocate for educational programs for their children.

Since that time, parent disability organizations have led the way in advocating for legislative reforms, educational services for children with disabilities, and policies leading to full inclusion of individuals with disabilities into society (Cunconan-Lahr & Brotherson, 1996; Powers, 1996). It has been argued that it is often the "synchrony of stakeholders" — influential parent insiders and parent and professional advocacy groups, among others — who come together at critical junctures to effect real systems change (A. P. Turnbull & Turnbull, 1996). In fact, in 1984, an influential U.S. Department of Education appointee as the Assistant to the Secretary for the

Office of Special Education and Rehabilitation Services, Madeline Will (herself a parent of a son with disabilities), opened the door for federal policies and practices impacting transition today.

Legal Requirements for Parent Participation

Since its inception, federal special education legislation has mandated a decision-making role for families as part of educational programs for students with disabilities. Current procedural due process provisions ensure accountability between schools and parents for safeguarding student rights under the Individuals With Disabilities Education Act of 2004 (IDEA; A. P. Turnbull, Turnbull, Erwin, & Soodak, 2006). In addition, parents have the right to access school records concerning their student and to determine who can have access to the records. These provisions give parents a controlling voice in the education and services of their children with disabilities. Parental involvement in systems-level decision making, program design, and governance is clearly required within IDEA's regulatory language (H. R. Turnbull, Stowe, & Huerta, 2007). IDEA ensures parent participation and advocacy at both the individual and systems levels; provisions related to parental participation on state and local special education advisory committees guarantees that their perspectives are incorporated into policy and program decisions and allows parents a voice at the systems level. (A. P. Turnbull, Turnbull, & Wehmeyer, 2007). IDEA sets the expectation that parents assume a leadership role in their children's transition planning process (Blue-Banning, Turnbull, & Pereira, 2002), although participation on advisory boards does not necessarily ensure that families will play critical roles in changing services and systems. Professionals and schools need to not only collaborate with but also empower parents in these roles.

What Is a Systems Change Agent?

What exactly does it mean to be a "systems change agent?" Some parents are committed to changing systems for their own child, whereas others take on the whole system. In either case, systems change agents work to change systems and services for an individual with disabilities or for a representative group with disabilities. Most parents and family members don't start out trying to change systems; in fact, most only want what's best for their child. However, their efforts result in changes in services, systems, policies, and practices that can impact all youth in the school district, the state, and the country. Indeed, it often takes just the power of one family wanting what's right for their child to effect the most significant changes. Once parents make a difference in their child's life by being systems change agents, they discover that their child is not the only one to benefit from change. An added benefit is that children with disabilities witness what their parents are doing and learn how to be advocates. They watch, learn, and start putting into practice what they see their parents do to make a difference.

For parents, making a difference for their child is satisfying. In fact, many parents have attested that the time, energy, and emotional costs of fighting the system were worth it to get what they needed. All of their

COMPETENCIES OF SYSTEMS CHANGE AGENTS

- Creating a vision for people with disabilities.

- Understanding how a bill becomes a law at the state and federal levels.

- Identifying critical federal issues and a process to personally address concerns.

- Demonstrating successful techniques for advocating for services to meet unserved and underserved individuals.

- Drafting and delivering testimony for legislative hearings.

- Meeting with public officials to express concerns.

- Identifying strategies for beginning and sustaining grassroots-level organizing.

- Using the media to effectively promote critical issues.

- Demonstrating proper procedures for conducting a meeting.

(Partners in Policymaking, n.d.).

efforts made a difference for their child, and some are satisfied that their job as systems change agent is done. For other parents, advocating for services for their child leads them to join with others and work alongside local, state, and national organizations to impact systemic change efforts.

Unfortunately, there is no magic formula that ensures successful systems change. Partners in Policymaking, a program designed to support families and consumers to develop personal advocacy and thereby impact disability policies and services, has identified characteristics such as creativity, tenacity, focus, vision, and negotiation skills as necessary to be successful change agents (n.d.; see box, "Competencies of Systems Change Agents"). School, community, and adult service systems that welcome parents as partners will develop strategic venues for parent voices to be central to their continuing efforts for system improvement. For those that do not, there are some determined parents who will continue to work as outsiders, advocating for change to meet the needs of their own children and others.

    Dwight's transformation from farmer to activist came about after completing the Partners in Policymaking program when he realized his son, Joel, then an eighth-grader, wasn't getting a good education. "The school didn't want to teach him math because the concepts were too confusing for him to learn. And they said that Joel was disruptive, that he couldn't sit still in the classroom." All that changed when Dwight and an occupational therapist solved Joel's seating solution. After winning the battle for appropriate educational experiences for his son, Dwight became a leader, teacher and supporter of other families. He started a support group for parents because he felt there was a need. He worked with a team to secure a grant to support families so that parents can find out about "what's out there for them to make life a little easier."

Minnesota Governor's Council on Developmental Disability, 2002, pp. 5–6

Systems Change for Families From Culturally and Linguistically Diverse Backgrounds

Other organizations have emerged to equip parents with the skills to advocate for their children. The Grassroots Consortium on Disabilities (http://www.gcod.org/) was formed in 1995 as a voice for community-based, parent-directed organizations serving culturally and linguistically diverse (CLD) families with children with disabilities from traditionally underserved areas. The services provided are individualized to meet the specific needs of the community. Grassroots works to develop community-based organizations through leadership development and advocacy efforts. The advocacy work of Grassroots members helped to launch U.S. Department of Education support for Community Parent Resource Centers (CPRCs). CPRCs are funded to provide parent training and information in targeted communities for underserved parents of children with disabilities, including low-income parents, parents of limited English proficient children, and parents with disabilities. CPRCs provide training and information to families about their rights, responsibilities, and protections under IDEA so that families can effectively participate in planning and decision making throughout their children's education.

Another organization, Fiesta Educativa (http://www.fiestaeducativa.org) was founded by family members and professionals in 1978 to specifically inform and assist Latino families in obtaining services and in caring for their children with special needs. Fiesta Educativa's family-based programs include conferences, parent support groups, community outreach, education and training, referral services, and research, among others. Their focus on systems change and leadership development includes the Marguerite Casey Foundation (http://www.caseygrants.org/), which trains and activates local parent leaders in low-income areas throughout California to become involved in legislation to affect systemic change.

Systems Change Agents During Transition

During transition, the active role of family members is an essential element to the success of students with disabilities. In many circumstances, once a student leaves school, the primary means of support, guidance, and advocacy falls to the family and the student's support network (Morningstar, Kleinhammer-Tramill, & Lattin, 1999; Newman, 2005). Parents are often the single most effective advocate for the child, and their efforts are critical for ensuring that school and adult services are not only available but align with the youth's vision for postschool life. Research supports the role of families in ensuring changes for positive transition outcomes. Specifically, high parental involvement has been associated with the achievement of postschool outcomes such as employment, postsecondary education, community living, and engagement in the community (Devlieger & Trach, 1999; Lindstrom, Doren, Metheny, Johnson, & Zane, 2007; Wagner, Newman, Cameto, Garza, & Levine, 2005). In fact, youth with disabilities have described the positive impact their families have played in ensuring successful adult lives after high school, particularly as it pertained to the development of specific career expectations (Lindstrom, Benz, & Doren, 2004;

Morningstar, 1997). In these circumstances, the role of parents is to ensure the availability of services that meet the needs and expectations of the child with disabilities; this often requires that they collaborate with others to develop innovative support systems (Minnesota Governor's Council on Developmental Disabilities, 2002). Sometimes it means that they work as systems change agents to advocate for programs and services beyond what are typically provided. In any case, the incentive and the goal become focused on improving school and postschool successes for youth. Often, that first foray into involvement through assisting their youth with their individual academic endeavors is the gateway for higher systems engagement levels in other aspects of their youth's services.

Although the impact of parental involvement on academic achievement has been the focus of research for adolescents in general (Epstein & Sheldon, 2006; Jeynes, 2007), it has not been thoroughly examined for youth with disabilities. However, research on parent engagement in school and transition activities is emerging from the National Longitudinal Transition Study 2 (NLTS2) parental survey data. Newman (2005) found that families reported moderate to high levels of engagement at home and in school-related transition activities, including regularly talking to their children; providing homework assistance; and participating in school meetings, parent–teacher conferences, and individualized education program (IEP) meetings. In addition, high levels of parental involvement appeared to promote youth achievement. The results indicated that students with highly engaged families have higher reading levels, receive better grades, are more involved with school-based groups, and report having more friends than families who are not as involved.

Many important questions about the relationship between parent engagement in school planning activities and student outcomes remain unanswered. Newman (2005) reported that whereas 9 out of 10 parents reported attending transition IEP meetings, only slightly more than half reported being involved in developing IEP goals, and one third wanted to be more involved in transition decision making. In addition, parental expectations for the future appear to affect postschool goal attainment, yet differing expectations between parents and school personnel can lead to increased efforts to ensure systems change (Thompson, Fulk, & Piercy, 2000).

This dilemma seems to be substantiated by NLTS2 data, in which parents report being less than equal participants during IEP and transition decision making and seeking to be more involved (Newman, 2005). This may be particularly true for families and youth from culturally and linguistically diverse backgrounds. Beliefs about adulthood, disability, and familial responsibility influence parental expectations and postsecondary goals for their children with disabilities (Geenen, Powers, Lopez-Vasquez, & Bersani, 2003; Rueda, Monzo, Shapiro, Gomez, & Blacher, 2005). Differing expectations for the future could lead to conflicts with transition professionals about what is considered to be appropriate transition services, thereby requiring family advocacy efforts. Murtadha-Watts and Stoughton (2004) found that after completion of special education assessments, professionals typically met to discuss the results, then came to an agreement on how they wanted to continue services; however, they did so without the parents' input. Consequently, this process caused parents to feel overpowered by professionals, uninformed about decisions, mistrusted, and uninvited. When parents are not treated as collaborative partners in planning for their child, they may take actions to confront the system so that they and their youth's preferences are central in the planning.

Given the importance of their role, parents must, in fact, become systems change agents in ever-expanding arenas including school, community, and agencies that offer adult services. Negotiating the maze of community services, funding streams, and eligibility requirements involves a new set of parental skills. This new arena also represents complex systems that could benefit from parental actions as systems change agents. Parents can work to address service difficulties by first considering what they want for their child, without focusing on current practice, policy, or what the school or agency will allow. Problem solving should start with asking questions such as "What's best for the student?" and "How can we make things work for this student to succeed in adult life?" These questions stimulate the team to collaborate and think outside the box. The next step is to work as a team to ameliorate school and agency constraints.

Challenges Parents Face as Systems Change Agents

Negative Practitioner Reactions

Unfortunately, strong parental advocacy doesn't always lead to positive relationships with the schools or agencies serving their children. Deborah McFadden, a former Commissioner of Developmental Disabilities for the U.S. Department of Health and Human Services, puts it this way: "Parents know best the needs of their children. But schools will often resist their suggestions . . . . The unfortunate truth is that if you are hated in your school system, you're probably doing a good job" (Shapiro, 1994, pg. 3). This statement rings true for parents who advocate during transition, as they are more likely to be perceived by professionals as "difficult" (Geenen et al., 2003; Morningstar et al., 1999). Resistance by practitioners may stem from a perception that school decisions should be made by the professionals or that the family is being unrealistic in their expectations. When parents are proactive, practitioners may become defensive. This in turn can result in families becoming more strident, and the cycle is likely to repeat itself, becoming increasingly confrontational (Wehmeyer, Morningstar, & Husted, 1999). Research suggests that professionals' negative attitudes have been barriers to involvement for CLD families during transition (Kim & Morningstar, 2005). Both practitioners and families may come to meetings with preconceptions that can interfere with collaborative transition planning.

History of Parent/School Conflicts and Mistrust

Changing an adversarial relationship can be hard, especially when parents and teachers have misjudged each other. Parents who have had negative experiences in the past may have difficulty trusting transition practitioners. This is often exacerbated for families from CLD backgrounds, including those from low socioeconomic backgrounds and parents who themselves had a difficult time in school. CLD parent involvement in school is considerably lower than that of European American families because of particular challenges such as poverty, language differences, limited resources, different beliefs about disabilities, and insufficient school support (Lynch & Hanson, 2004; Zhang & Benz, 2006). Unfortunately, many educators have not considered the specific circumstances and how they might affect the CLD families' involvement in transition planning (Geenen, Powers, & Lopez-Vasquez, 2001). As a result, CLD parents are often less involved in formal and school-based transition planning; establishing trust between parents and schools or agencies early on during transition planning is an important first task. Finding ways for all stakeholders to work together as partners and create new ways to support youth as they move into adulthood is at the heart of collaborative systems change.

Lack of Knowledge About Transition and Advocacy

Limited knowledge of what to expect after high school is not a new fear for families. Empowering families requires that they have access to relevant information; A. P. Turnbull et al (2006) have indicated that specific information families want includes service availability, community resources, and parenting practices. These researchers indicated that access to information is one of the greatest unmet needs of families. However, families differ in their preferences for how they want to access information. Transition meetings often include a myriad of new people and new realms of information, which can be hard for families to digest all at once. In addition, families may be struggling with emotional issues surrounding their children's transition to adulthood. Therefore, it is critical that practitioners provide consistent and relevant information over extended periods of time and in a variety of formats for families, heeding the warnings of one parent: "It's not simply that people aren't getting enough information, it's why they are not getting it when they want it or in the form they can absorb . . . . So it's not enough for services to simply chuck the leaflets across the table" (A. P. Turnbull et al., 2006, pg. 216).

Confusion and Trepidation About Roles

Families may be apprehensive about how much of a difference they can make in a large or cumbersome system. This is particularly true during the transition from school to adult life, when families move out of the special education service system where children with disabilities are entitled to a free and appropriate public education. Adult agencies operate from an eligibility perspective, and parents must learn the eligibility requirements and application procedures for each agency that serves their young adult. When facing the daunting task of changing an established system, parents report uncertainty about their roles, cultural barriers, and lack of supportive environments for participation (Blue-Banning et al., 2002; deFur, Todd-Allen, & Getzel, 2001; Kim & Morningstar, 2005). Family members and educators often have differing perceptions of the best way for parents to be involved with school and community systems improvement. For example, teachers may think the best way for parents to be involved is by attending school meetings, whereas parents may see themselves contributing by supporting their child at home in more personalized ways (Geenen et al., 2003). Very few parents would independently see themselves in a role of changing systems that they are just coming to understand.

Isolation and Disempowerment

Given work and family commitments, especially when exacerbated by the presence of a disability in the family (A. P. Turnbull et al., 2006), it may take an extraordinary commitment for parents to prioritize systems change activities into their lives. In fact, as children move through the middle school years and into high school, families in general and those with adolescents with disabilities in particular may become isolated and disconnected from school and the community (Ruef & Turnbull, 2001; Sanders & Herting, 2000). This may result in feeling that they have no control over an unfamiliar system. For families from CLD backgrounds, feelings of distrust may be pronounced. Rueda and colleagues (2005) indentified four themes regarding professionals' attitudes that resulted in negative interactions with families: (a) poor communication with families, (b) lack of effort in providing services, (c) negative attitude to towards children they were serving, and (d) negative treatment of parents. As a result, parents felt a lack of trust towards the educators. Under these circumstances, rather than feeling accepted and capable of advocating for their child, the parents felt alienated within the adversarial climate. Creating positive partnerships with families can alleviate family isolation. It requires building on strengths, talents, resources and expertise of both educators and families (A.P. Turnbull et al., 2007).

> ❝ We don't need to bash or blame professionals for everything. We're going to have to come together and work in the best interests of our kids. Professionals are going to need the commitment families have. It might mean asking the professionals to stand in the family's shoes and ask themselves the question, If this were my family, what would I want to see happen? ❞
>
> *A. Turnbull & Turnbull, 2006, p. 349*

Strategies Supporting Systems Change Agents During Transition

Systems Change at the "My Child" Level

There are a number of strategies that practitioners can implement to support parents in their individual advocacy role focusing on the "my child" level. Remembering that most advances in special education law and practice have been the result of parents who saw something missing for their children and took a stand to confront the system, practitioners can work to build a safe space for parents to advocate for change within the system.

Strengthen parent and family leadership skills. Most parent advocates say that it takes a combination of motivation and skills to make change happen (A. P. Turnbull et al., 2006). Parents and individuals with disabilities involved with Partners in Policymaking identified three critical skills needed to be an effective advocate:

1. *Empowering voices*—learning how to communicate effectively and with whom; knowing what to say and when to say it.

2. *Networking with others*—recognizing your personal skills and characteristics and turning to family and friends for support.

3. *Courage*—being "willing to stick your neck out for what you believe in even though people may not follow ... courage is required daily." (Cunconan-Lahr & Brotherson, 1996, pg. 355)

Partners in Policymaking (www.partnersinpolicymaking.com) was created by the Minnesota Governor's Council on Developmental Disabilities in 1987 and since that time it has offered a leadership training program, with workshops in many states, designed to teach parents and self-advocates the power of advocacy leading to systems change. More than 15,000 Partners graduates are part of a growing national network of community leaders serving on policy-making committees, commissions, and boards at local, state, and national levels. More recently, Partners has created online courses available to anyone interested in learning how to become a change agent.

Partners is the only national training program that is designed to specifically train parents and individuals with disabilities together. Participants learn from nationally known speakers about the history of services for individuals with developmental disabilities as well as state-of-art policies and practices (e.g., community living, supported employment, inclusive education, whole life planning). This combination allows advocates to develop a vision for their future and for others they might be advocating for, thereby ensuring high levels of systems change.

Partners graduates gain effective strategies for systems change by learning how state and federal policies are formulated, how to deliver testimony for legislative hearings, how to meet with public officials, how to use media to promote issues, and strategies for grassroots organizing. Upon graduating from the program, participants choose a community project to implement—one which will improve the quality of lives of people with disabilities in their home community, a true sign of a well-trained systems change agent (or, as Ed Roberts so astutely described, "Upon graduation, Partners become members of the 'Giraffe Society' because they're willing to stick out their necks"; 1987).

A recent study of Partners in Policymaking graduates reported their involvement in significant changes related to housing, education, employment, case management, friendships, and health care. This included parental involvement in ensuring inclusive education for their children, advocating for their child's enrollment in postsecondary programs, and increased community employment for their adult children. Other forms of change impacted by parents included increased in-home and personal care support services, creating better housing options for adults, and improved health care services. These graduates reported that they learned critical skills for advocacy that they used in their daily lives including legislative advocacy, self-advocacy, communication skills, self-confidence, negotiation skills, leadership, and networking (Nichols, 2007).

Transition practitioners can support families' development of leadership skills by offering written information, sponsoring workshops, and by connecting family members with others who are effective advocates and change agents. School and adult services agencies can support networking by sponsoring a family involvement and advocacy subcommittee for a transition fair, where families can learn about transition planning, hear from adult agencies, and meet with other families also going through transition. Finally, one of the most important ways professionals can support effective family advocacy is to respond appropriately and empathetically to families who are learning these skills. Professionals themselves need to understand how to effectively communicate with families and model these skills with families.

Help students and family members to develop a vision for the future.
During the transition process, parents may become change agents because they, along with their adolescent, possess a vision for the future that is, according to Ann Turnbull (Co-Director of the Beach Center on Disability, a national family research center), an "enviable lifestyle" (1995). Such a vision for the future often focuses on inclusion in school, employment, and the community at large. Most important, the vision is based on hopes that, as a result of their school experiences, these youth will have developed personal advocacy and self-determination skills. In order to achieve this quality adult life, new ways to support individuals with disabilities in the community as emergent self-advocates need to be developed above and beyond what schools or agencies have traditionally provided. However, for other parents, the specific vision for their youth's future is less clear. Although they may not have fully considered their son's or daughter's adult life, they do know that the current "disability menu" available at any one agency is not what they want for their child. This may be all that is needed to take them down the road to becoming an advocate for change.

> When I participated in [New Hampshire] Leadership, my daughter was only three years old and in a self-contained preschool program. Leadership was my first serious lesson in "Standing Up For What Is Right 101." I gained confidence in my ability to be an advocate for my daughter, acquired knowledge about what all the possibilities are for people with disabilities, and made the friends I need for support. Following my Leadership experience, we advocated for our daughter to be placed in a typical preschool program, and she was! At the middle school level, we had to advocate for our daughter to be placed in the general curriculum program and be graded like her peers, and she was! Marika is in high school now, working toward a scholastic diploma, despite the many challenges she faces because of cerebral palsy. Although she uses a wheelchair for mobility and augmentative communication devices, she will enroll in the Driver's Education program in the fall. This summer, Marika has been interviewing for a part-time job in the health services field . . . . Leadership showed me how to stand up for her rights and teach her to stand up for herself. Her education, social life, and community experiences have all been positively influenced by what I learned in Leadership.
>
> *New Hampshire Leadership, n.d.*

The early waves of NLTS2 parent data indicate that, in general, families have high expectations for the future. For example, the majority of parents (85%) expected their children to graduate from high school with a regular diploma and live independently (Newman, 2005). In addition, almost two thirds of the parents reported they envisioned their child in a postsecondary school setting (i.e., vocational/technical school, community college, 4-year college). Most parents "definitely or probably" expected their child to live independently (84%) and to be financially self-supporting (82%). However, these expectations varied by type of disability, with parents of students classified with more significant disabilities having lower expectations than those with mild disabilities. However, certain groups of families still possessed a limited views for the future, including parents of youth from low-income households; only 41% of parents from households with incomes of $25,000 or less expected their children to "definitely" graduate from high school, compared with 63% of those with incomes over $50,000. Such lowered expectations may reflect lower graduation rates found in many schools with large proportions of low-income students. Mirroring income differences, parents' expectations for graduation and postschool outcomes were higher for European American youth with disabilities than for parents from other ethnic/racial backgrounds. For example, 56% of European American parents expected their children to "definitely" graduate with a regular diploma, compared with 48% of African American students (Newman).

In light of the implications of these NLTS2 data, practitioners should work with parents and students before, during, and after transition meetings to ensure a focus on the student's postschool goals and preparation for transition to adulthood. This should involve providing current and useful information to families when they need it. The Technical Assistance on Transition and the Rehabilitation Act (TATRA) Project (PACER, 2008) is an excellent source for current information to help families prepare youth with disabilities for their future. TATRA provides information and training on transition planning, the adult service system, and strategies that prepare youth for successful employment, postsecondary education, and independent living outcomes. Providing information about current and future services, community resources, and legal rights helps families to develop trusting and positive relationships with professionals (Park & Turnbull, 2001; A. P. Turnbull et al., 2006). To understand what families want and need regarding future expectations, practitioners should turn to already established infrastructures to support families such as the National Alliance for Parent Training and Information Centers (http://www.taalliance.org). Ultimately, practitioners should critically sift through the overwhelming abundance of information, online and in print, and point families and youth towards relevant information that they need to solidify their vision of the future and determine appropriate pathways and resources towards achieving that vision.

To help families and students with disabilities achieve their goals, schools and adult agencies need to offer specifically tailored planning structures. Person-centered planning is one very successful way to support families and youth in developing a meaningful vision for their future as adults. Indeed, person-centered planning methods, which incorporate new and innovative means of support, were developed specifically to help families and individuals with disabilities to develop a vision for the future. This planning approach also supports families and individuals in identifying service changes necessary to put this vision into action (Holburn & Vietze, 2002).

Meaningful changes in services and systems can occur more quickly if parents and professionals come together in new ways to plan for the future and to create a plan of action that leads to change. For transition practitioners and adult service providers, this involves developing a transition planning process that changes the way transition meetings are held to ensure (a) that a vision for the future is at the core of the transition plan and (b) that families and youth are supported in achieving their vision through transition services available in school and the community. The vision for the future should not be driven by the traditional services that may be currently offered. In fact, if innovative services and supports are not yet available in a community, then transition professionals must work in partnership with families and adult agencies to change the way adults are supported in the community. Keeping informed of new policies and initiatives (e.g., Ticket to Work and Work Incentives Improvement Act of 1999, Home and Community-Based Services Medicaid waivers, individualized funding systems, and wrap-around services) is an important role for educators and service providers. Sharing information about these new programs with families is an essential part of supporting families to identify and take action towards their vision.

Researchers investigating how parents and individuals with disabilities develop into systems change agents have stressed that the "role of the advocate must be understood in terms of its supports and barriers, but also as a vision and passion relative to one's personal beliefs" (Cunconan-Lahr & Brotherson, 1996, p. 357). These characteristics are motivating and guiding forces for supporting families and youth to make needed changes; transition professionals must develop an understanding and respect for families' and students' personal strengths, contributions, and cultural values impacting their vision for the future.

Build trusting relationships with families. Parents have reported that good relationships and effective communication with professionals promoted their participation in the transition process (Geenen et al., 2003; Wehmeyer, et al., 1999). Consequently, relationships and interactions with school professionals have been identified as a pivotal factor in partnerships during transition (deFur et al, 2001; Kim & Morningstar, 2005). Unfortunately, special education practitioners often do not have the knowledge and skills needed to collaborate effectively with parents (A. P. Turnbull et al., 2006). At the secondary level, one reason identified as contributing to this barrier is inadequate attention within teacher education programs (Morningstar & Kleinhammer-Tramill, 2005; Shartrand, Weiss, Kreider, & Lopez, 1997; Szymanski, 1994). The lack of information about parental involvement strategies may be compounded when secondary special education teachers and CLD parents need to jointly plan for a student's future (Greenen et al., 2003; Hoover-Dempsey, Walker, Jones, & Reed, 2002).

Indeed, the attitudes of teachers have been found to be closely related to their level of active engagement with parents (Epstein, 2001; Garcia, 2004): Teachers who perceive themselves as more efficacious in their ability to work with families make more attempts to involve families in the educational process (Hoover-Dempsey et al., 2002). Furthermore, teachers who have learned the value of parent involvement are more likely to persist in overcoming barriers and obstacles to establish positive interactions (Becker & Epstein, 1982). Finally, teachers who involve parents are much less likely to form negative stereotypes about parents and families, and the more often teachers interact with parents, the more positive their attitudes are toward parent involvement and listening to parental input (Epstein).

INDICATORS OF SUCCESS FOR EFFECTIVE PRACTICES IN SUPPORT OF PARENTS AS SYSTEMS CHANGE AGENTS AT THE "MY CHILD" LEVEL

○ Practitioners share information about research-based transition practices and models with parents to enlighten families about new ways to provide services and to enlist their support as new programs are developed.

○ Transition information is offered to parents in many formats across time, not just during a single point in time such as the IEP meeting.

○ Teams use person-centered methods for planning prior to and during the IEP meeting to build youth's ownership of his own transition vision and plan and to encourage their motivation, self-efficacy, persistence, and vision for the future.

○ Practitioners and parents share information about community agencies and systems as well as local and state initiatives, opening discussion about both the opportunities and gaps.

○ Practitioners, youth, and families collaboratively problem solve unique solutions to the youth's transition support needs, and effectively communicate their points of view.

○ Families are encouraged to connect with others in similar circumstances, such as support groups and/or advocacy organizations.

Systems Change at Local and State Levels

Inviting involvement on school decision-making teams. Professionals can and should invite parents to participate in school-based governance teams and offer support to families to ensure an active and meaningful role. Parental involvement in systems-level decision making and governance is one of the six principles of IDEA (H. R. Turnbull et al., 2007). Involving families of children and youth with disabilities on school councils and special education advisory boards is both required by law and also an important way to ensure parent advocacy at the systems level; however, many schools, especially middle and high schools, continue to resist the idea of parental involvement on governance committees (Henderson & Raimondo, 2001). Establishing trusting relationships with families is extremely important because it cultivates positive partnerships that can impact school and district services (A. P. Turnbull et al., 2006). However, some parents develop feelings of mistrust during meetings because they may feel powerless and unheard (Landmark, Zhang, & Montoya, 2007; Murtadha-Watts & Stoughton, 2004).

" Rijuta Pathre is on many boards and committees, including the state Special Education Advisory Council (SEAC). "We talk about policy, we make changes, and we see the results of those changes," Rijuta says. "I'm involved in the policy end because that's where everything starts. Citizens really do have a voice, and they can indeed make a difference. People say, 'You're just one person; you can't change the system.' Well, you can change the system." "

Minnesota Governor's Council on Developmental Disability, 2002, pp. 67–69

For parents of students with disabilities, involvement in school governance, site-based management, and other decision-making processes is not often evident (McLaughlin, Henderson, & Rhim, 1998). Research has shown that it is possible to increase parental involvement at the secondary level, even with those from poor or minority families (Sanders, Epstein, & Connors-Tadros, 1999). If schools encourage partnerships with parents on decision-making committees, more families will become involved in school-based activities. In fact, family attitudes and involvement in school are positively influenced by such efforts. More outreach efforts have been integrated into practices in special education and transition, and the initial results are encouraging. In fact, parents of youth with disabilities reported that school decision making is a critical role for them and one about which they want more information (Newman, 2005; Pleet, Ripley, & McKelvey-Chik, 2000).

If secondary schools are to enhance parent participation on site-based committees, then transition professionals must offer parents the information and support they need to become effective partners. Family involvement is more than mere attendance at a meeting. Educators can facilitate family involvement during transition by (a) asking families how they want to be involved and respecting this expressed level of involvement; (b) creating comprehensive school programs that incorporate the role of families as decision makers; (c) viewing extended family members as potential contributors; and (d) helping families and students connect with needed community services (Wehmeyer et al., 1999). When parents have become comfortable with participating on committees and boards, they may decide to expand their influence beyond evaluator and decision maker into systems change agent. That is when their valuable perspectives can truly impact the system.

Supporting parents as change agents on system reform efforts. The responsibilities and burdens of gaining knowledge and skills to make effective decisions in this era of school reform and No Child Left Behind Act of 2001 (NCLB) accountability measures may seem overwhelming, especially for parents who are often not a part of the reform decision-making process. The IDEA 2004 amendments included regulatory language requiring that all students with disabilities be provided supports and modifications to ensure their progress in the general curriculum. Parents are required members of IEP teams where decisions are made about a student's educational program and his or her progress in the general curriculum. In a recent review of the role of families in standards-based educational reform, Morningstar (2003) identified multiple challenges to actively engaging families of youth with disabilities in such decisions. One noteworthy barrier to parental involvement is the general lack of commitment among schools to enhance parental involvement beyond rudimentary roles. In addition, special educators as well as parents are often left out of school-based planning efforts involving school reform decisions. Finally, some parents and special educators are fearful that students with disabilities will lose rights and safeguards under IDEA. For example, parents who sit on school improvement committees will need support in order to effectively consider the overall impact of access to the general curriculum on student needs and accommodations, as well as the impact of inclusion in state and local accountability systems. Such new roles and decisions required of families will most certainly place even greater demands on parents to make informed decisions about students with disabilities' access to the general curriculum.

An encouraging sign is the growth in information and resources available for parents that are "usable to the extreme" (Thurlow, Elliott, & Ysseldyke, 1998, p. v). One source for information about school reform is the Parent Information Resource Center program (PIRC; http://www.nationalpirc.org). With funding from the U.S. Department of Education, more than 80 PIRCs are working to inform and educate parents, family advocates, educators, community organizers, and others who are committed to educational success for all students, especially low-income, minority, and English language learning students. NCLB expanded parents' roles in school accountability in two ways: by giving them greater choice over the schools their children attend, and mandating extra help for struggling students. NCLB placed more responsibility on all parents, including those with children with disabilities and PIRCs offer parent-friendly information so they can make effective choices and decisions. PIRCs help implement effective parental involvement policies, programs, and activities leading to student achievement by strengthening partnerships among parents, teachers, principals, administrators, and other school personnel. These state and regional organizations engage in technical assistance including helping parents understand state and district accountability systems and providing information to parents about the significance of accountability data for opportunities available to families including supplemental services and public school choice. PIRCs work closely with the disability-specific parent information and training centers to better serve all students.

It is imperative that teachers and other support personnel (e.g., social workers, transition coordinators, guidance counselors) are knowledgeable about the systems change efforts taking place in schools and can communicate these efforts to families of youth with disabilities. Families need general information about the intent of school-reform efforts, how NCLB affects their children, and how their children can increase academic and functional achievement while in school. Families of youth with disabilities can and should be involved in this process, particularly as members of site-based management teams. Therefore, special educators also need to advocate that families of students with disabilities be involved and included on such state, district, and local decision-making boards.

Involvement in state and community transition teams. Parents who want to impact systems change beyond advocating for changes in services only for their son or daughter can become involved in school and district transition advisory groups and communitywide transition planning efforts. Community or local transition teams focus on the services and supports in a community that are provided for students in transition from school to adult life. These teams work toward making improvements in services, creating new services, and educating students, families, and the community about the transition process. At the state level, councils or teams usually focus on statewide transition services, policies, and programs as well as on the general needs of local transition teams. An excellent resource for state community transition teams is the Transition Community of Practice on Shared Work (www.sharedwork.org).

A valuable role for parents with youth with disabilities is to become active on a community transition team (CTT). A CTT is a group of individuals who have an active interest in ensuring that students with disabilities have opportunities to achieve the futures they see for themselves (Morningstar et al., 2007). Most CTTs include of a variety of people (e.g., students with disabilities, family members, school personnel, adult service agency personnel, employers, community members) and meet regularly to develop ways to meet transition planning needs in their communities. Halpern, Benz, and Lindstrom (1992) and colleagues described the purpose of local transition teams as

> to discover and implement new and better ways of providing secondary special education and transition services. . . . The essence of the transition councils . . . is that they function at the local level, taking advantage of the unique strengths of their own communities while working to solve common problems. (p. 1)

CTTs assess, plan, and implement changes in transition services (Blalock & Benz, 1999). Although it is essential that parents be involved, this is easier said than done. Even teams that are considered to be extremely active often express difficulty in involving parents (Lattin & Anderson, 1999). As with other forms of communitywide change efforts, barriers to parental involvement must be addressed in order to ensure their participation. Strategies for increasing parental involvement on community transition teams include increasing publicity and direct contact with parents to inform them of activities and events, offering food and child care, and scheduling meetings during times when families are more likely to attend.

Parents play an important role on CTTs by helping to identify the critical transition needs of the community. This can be accomplished by including families in planning meetings as well as soliciting input from all parents of students in transition. Some communities use a needs assessment survey to include a wide variety of parental input. Parents should also be involved in formulating action goals for the team. They can be instrumental in ensuring that community transition team activities will effectively meet the needs of parents. Often, this includes team action planning to develop information and resources specifically for families, such as community resource directories, brochures, and Web sites. Parents can also work with the community transition team to organize and host transition fairs, conferences, and workshops specifically for families. Involving parents throughout the planning and implementation will ensure that activities are meaningful to families and will increase the likelihood that other parents will attend and become involved in the activities.

INDICATORS OF SUCCESS FOR EFFECTIVE PRACTICES IN SUPPORT OF PARENTS AS SYSTEMS CHANGE AGENT AT THE LOCAL AND STATE SYSTEMS LEVEL

○ Families participate in school-based, community, and state-level decision-making groups.

○ Families are supported as systems advocates by providing information, skill-building, networking with other families, child care for meetings, and meetings scheduled at convenient times for families.

○ School policies ensure families of youth with disabilities are included in parent advisory groups and school governance committees.

○ Practitioners invite and support families to play meaningful roles on community transition teams to effect changes in services for youth and adults with disabilities.

○ Transition professionals and schools respect families who choose formal processes for advocating for changes and cooperate with such processes to avoid adversarial relationships.

Partnering with parents in advocating for changes. Transition practitioners typically do not consider how they can partner with parents and youth with disabilities in advocating for changes, particularly within a school environment. Teachers and other school professionals often find it difficult to directly advocate within the system where they are employed. Practitioners may have experienced the frustrations of trying to make changes from within the system, to no avail.

An effective strategy for educators wanting to impact systems change is to partner with families by offering resources, examples of innovative programs, information about existing parental advocacy organizations and individual parent advocates who will support them in meetings and other settings, and help them network with other parents who are in advocacy roles. In this way, education and transition professionals can support families to advocate for themselves, a proactive and positive way to effect change. A. P. Turnbull and colleagues (2006) posit that to empower parents, professionals should develop programs to engage in advocacy along with and on behalf of parents—thereby creating the balance of power necessary for all parents to be empowered.

Conclusion

Parents often describe becoming an advocate as a life-changing event; others emphasize the stress that comes with being the one to advocate for something new. Whatever the circumstances, it is clear that without parents in the role of systems change agent, the degree of changes in services and systems would not be as extensive as they are today. During the transition to adulthood, parents often are required to be systems change agents, particularly if they have a vision of an inclusive adult life for their sons and daughters with disabilities. There will always be parents who develop a commitment to take action to change the system. With expanding resources and organizations to support them, their numbers are growing. They may be speaking for their own child or for many. Transition practitioners and systems have the choice of establishing a place for parent voice at the planning table, committed to actively listening to their views of what's missing in the current system. Pursuing historic patterns of operating as though parents are outsiders will result in these parents using other less collaborative means to impact the system: formal complaints, hearings, testimony, and class action lawsuits. They will not be silent, and future generations will profit from their actions.

REFERENCES

Becker, H. J., & Epstein, J. L. (1982). Parent involvement: A study of teacher practices. *Elementary School Journal, 83,* 85–102.

Blalock, G., & Benz, M. (1999). *Using community transition teams to improve transition services.* Austin, TX: Pro-Ed.

Blue-Banning, M., Turnbull, A. P., & Pereira, L. (2002). Hispanic youth/young adults with disabilities: Parents' visions for the future. *Research and Practice for Persons with Severe Disabilities, 27,* 204–219.

Cunconan-Lahr, R., & Brotherson, M. J. (1996). Advocacy in disability policy: Parents and consumers as advocates. *Mental Retardation, 34,* 352–358.

deFur, S. H., Todd-Allen, M., & Getzel, E. E. (2001). Parent participation in the transition planning process. *Career Development for Exceptional Individuals, 24,* 19–36.

Devlieger, P. J., & Trach, J. S. (1999). Mediation as a transition process: The impact on postschool employment outcomes. *Exceptional Children, 65,* 507–523.

Epstein, J. L. (2001). *School, family, and community partnerships: Preparing educators and improving schools.* Boulder, CO: Westview Press.

Epstein, J. L., & Sheldon, S. B. (2006). Moving foward: Ideas for research on school, family, and community partnerships. In C. F. Conrad & R. C. Serlin (Eds.), *The SAGE handbook for research in education: Engaging ideas and enriching inquiry* (pp. 117–137). Thousand Oaks, CA: Sage.

Garcia, D. C. (2004). Exploring connections between the construct of teacher efficacy and family involvement practices: Implications for urban teacher preparation. *Urban Education, 39,* 290–315.

Geenen, S., Powers, L., & Lopez-Vasquez, A. (2001). Multicultural aspects of parent involvement in transition planning. *Exceptional Children, 67,* 265–282.

Geenen, S., Powers, L. E., Lopez-Vasquez, A., & Bersani, H. (2003). Understanding and promoting the transition of minority adolescents. *Career Development for Exceptional Individuals, 26,* 27 46.

Halpern, A. S., Benz, M. R., & Lindstrom, L. E. (1992). A systems change approach to improving secondary special education and transition programs at the community level. *Career Development for Exceptional Individuals, 15,* 109–120.

Henderson, A. T., & Raimondo, B. N. (2001). Unlocking parent potential. *Principal Leadership, 2*(1), 26–32.

Holburn, S., & Vietze, P. (2002). *Person-centered planning: Research, practice, and future directions.* Baltimore, MD: Paul H. Brookes.

Hoover-Dempsey, K. V., Walker, J. M. T., Jones, K. P., & Reed, R. P. (2002). Teachers involving parents (TIP): Results of an in-service teacher education program for enhancing parental involvement. *Teaching and Teacher Education, 18,* 843–867.

Jeynes, W. H. (2007). The relationship between parental involvement and urban secondary school student academic achievement: A meta-analysis. *Urban Education, 42*(1), 82–110.

Kim, K., & Morningstar, M. (2005). Transition planning involving culturally and linguistically diverse families. *Career Development for Exceptional Individuals, 28,* 92–103.

Landmark, L., Zhang, D., & Montoya, L. (2007). Culturally diverse parents' experiences in their children's transition: Knowledge and involvement. *Career Development for Exceptional Individuals, 30,* 68–79.

Lattin, D. L., & Anderson, K. (1999). *Kansas transition council annual report.* Lawrence: University of Kansas.

Lindstrom, L., Benz, M. R., & Doren, B. (2004). Expanding career options for young women with disabilities. *Career Development for Exceptional Individuals, 27,* 43–63.

Lindstrom, L., Doren, B., Metheny, J., Johnson, P., & Zane, C. (2007). Transition to employment: Role of the family in career development. *Exceptional Children, 73,* 348–366.

Lynch, E. W., & Hanson, M. J. (2004). *A guide for working with children and their families: Developing cross-cultural competence* (3rd ed.). Baltimore: Brookes.

McLaughlin, M. J., Henderson, K., & Rhim, L. M. (1998, September). *Snapshots of reform: How five local districts are interpreting standards-based reform for students with disabilities.* Alexandria, VA: Center for Policy Research on the Impact of General and Special Education Reform.

Minnesota Governor's Council on Developmental Disabilities. (2002). *Stories of leadership.* Minneapolis, MN: Author.

Morningstar, M. E. (1997). Critical issues in career development and employment practices for adolescents with disabilities. *Remedial and Special Education, 18,* 307–320.

Morningstar, M. E. (2003). The role of families of adolescents with disabilities in standards-based educational reform and transition. In C. A. Kochhar-Bryant & D. S. Bassett (Eds.), *Aligning transition and standards-based education: Issues and strategies* (pp. 125–150). Arlington, VA: Council for Exceptional Children.

Morningstar, M. E., & Kleinhammer-Tramill, P. J. (2005). *Professional development for transition personnel: current issues and strategies for success* (National Center on Secondary Education and Transition Information Brief). Minneapolis: University of Minnesota.

Morningstar, M. E., Kleinhammer-Tramill, P. J., & Lattin, D. L. (1999). Using successful models of student-centered transition planning and services for adolescents with disabilities. *Focus on Exceptional Children, 31*(9), 1–19.

Morningstar, M. E., Noonan, P. M., Lattin, D. L., Clavenna-Deane, B., Pearson, M., & Soukup, J. (2007). *Arizona community transition teams training: Developing comprehensive community-wide transition systems to improve results.* Lawrence: University of Kansas.

Murtadha-Watts, K., & Stoughton, E. (2004). Critical cultural knowledge in special education: Reshaping the responsiveness of school leaders. *Focus on Exceptional Children, 37*(2), 1–8.

New Hampshire Leadership. (n.d.). *Graduate profiles.* Retrieved November 20, 2008, from http://nhleadership.org/graduate.html

Newman, L. (2005). *Family involvement in the educational development of youth with disabilities. A special topic report from the National Longitudinal Transition Study-2 (NLTS2).* Menlo Park, CA: SRI International.

Nichols, M. J. (2007, June). *Partners in Policymaiking longitudinal study.* Retrieved October 21, 2008, from http://www.partnersinpolicymaking.com/index.html

PACER Center. (2008). *Technical assistance on transition and the rehabilitation act.* Bloomington, MN: Author. Available http://www.pacer.org/tatra/

Park, J., & Turnbull, A. P. (2001). Cross-cultural competency and special education: Perceptions and experiences of Korean parents of children with special needs. *Education and Training in Mental Retardation and Developmental Disabilities 36,* 133–147.

Partners in Policymaking. (n.d.). *Curriculum highlights: Systems change.* Minneapolis: Minnesota Governor's Council on Developmental Disabilities. Retrieved October 8, 2008, from http://www.partnersinpolicymaking.com/curriculumchange.html

Pleet, A., Ripley, S., & McKelvey-Chik, L. (2000, April 25). *Partnering with parents of youth with disabilities.* Transcript of conference call presentation, National Transition Alliance. Retrieved January 22, 2007, from http://www.dssc.org/nta/html/index_2.htm

Powers, L. (1996). Family and consumer activism in disability policy. In G. Singer, L. Powers, & A. Olson (Eds.), *Redefining family support* (pp. 413–434). Baltimore, MD: Paul H. Brookes.

Roberts, E. (Speaker). (1987, May). *Effective Strategies for Social Change* [Video]. Minneapolis: Minnesota Governor's Council on Developmental Disabilities. Available from http://www.mnddc.org/parallels2/one/video/ed_roberts-pipm.html

Rueda, R., Monzo, L., Shapiro, J., Gomez, J., & Blacher, J. (2005). Cultural models of transition: Latina mothers of young adults with developmental disabilities. *Exceptional Children, 71,* 401–414.

Ruef, M. D., & Turnbull, A. P. (2001). Stakeholder opinions on accessible informational products helpful in building positive, practical solutions to behavioral challenges of individuals with mental retardation and/or autism. *Education and Training in Mental Retardation and Developmental Disabilities, 36,* 441–456.

Sanders, M. G., Epstein, J. L., & Connors-Tadros, L. (1999, February). *Family partnerships with high schools: The parents' perspective* (Report No. 32). Baltimore: Johns Hopkins University Center for Research on Education of Students Placed at Risk. Retrieved September, 21, 2001, from http://www.csos.jhu.edu/crespar/Reports/report32.pdf

Sanders, M. G., & Herting, J. R. (2000). Gender and the effects of school, family, and church support on the academic achievement of African-American urban adolescents. In M. G. Sanders (Ed.), *Schooling students placed at risk: Research, policy and practice in the education of poor and minority adolescents* (pp.141–162). Mahwah, NJ: Lawrence Erlbaum.

Shapiro, J. P. (1994, January, 10). The mothers of invention: How a mighty grassroots movement of parents with disabled kids is changing the nation. *U.S. News and World Report.* Retrieved January 24, 2002, from http://www.usnews.com/usnews/news/articles/940110/archive_012209.htm

Shartrand, A. M., Weiss, H. B., Kreider, H. M., & Lopez, M. E. (1997). *New skills for new schools: Preparing teachers in family involvement.* Cambridge, MA: Harvard Family Research Project.

Szymanski, E. M. (1994). Transition: Life-span, life-space considerations for empowerment. *Exceptional Children, 60,* 402–410.

Thompson, J. R., Fulk, B. M., & Piercy, S. W. (2000). Do individualized transition plans match the postschool projections of students with learning disabilities and their parents? *Career Development for Exceptional Individuals, 23,* 3–25.

Thurlow, M. L., Elliott, J. L., & Ysseldyke, J. E. (1998). *Testing students with disabilities: Practical strategies for complying with district and state requirements.* Thousand Oaks, CA: Corwin Press.

Turnbull, A. (1995, July). Keynote address to the National Conference of the Autism Society of America, Greensboro, North Carolina.

Turnbull, A. P., & Turnbull, H. R. (1996) The synchrony of stakeholders. In S. L. Kagan & N. E. Cohen (Eds.), *Reinventing early care and education* (pp. 209–305). San Francisco: Jossey-Bass.

Turnbull, A. P., Turnbull, H. R, Erwin, E., & Soodak, L. (2006). *Families, professionals, and exceptionality: Positive outcomes through partnerships* (5th ed.). Upper Saddle River, NJ: Merrill Prentice Hall.

Turnbull, A. P., Turnbull, H. R., & Wehmeyer, M. (2007). *Exceptional lives: Special education in today's schools* (5th ed.). Upper Saddle River, NJ: Merrill Prentice Hall.

Turnbull H. R., Stowe, M. J., & Huerta, N. E. (2007). *Free appropriate public education: The law and children with disabilities* (7th ed.). Denver, CO: Love.

Wagner, M., Newman, L., Cameto, R., Garza, N., & Levine, P. (2005). *After high school: A first look at the postschool experiences of youth with disabilities.* Menlo Park, CA: SRI International.

Wehmeyer, M. L., Morningstar, M. E., & Husted, D. (1999). *Family involvement in transition planning and implementation.* Austin, TX: Pro-Ed.

Zhang, D., & Benz, M. R. (2006). Enhancing self-determination of culturally diverse students with disabilities: Current status and future challenges. *Focus on Exceptional Children, 38*(9), 1–12.

ABOUT THE AUTHOR

MARY E. MORNINGSTAR is an Associate Professor in the Department of Special Education at the University of Kansas and Director of the Transition Coalition, which offers national transition professional development through online training and technical assistance. Her research interests include professional development and teacher training in the area of transition, supporting families during transition, particularly those from culturally and linguistically diverse backgrounds, and supporting students with significant disabilities during transition.

8

Strategic Engagement for Parent Partnerships

Donna L. Wandry and Amy M. Pleet

ESSENTIAL QUESTIONS

○ How can schools and agencies measure the effectiveness of strategies to build parent partnerships?

○ What priorities should guide strategic expansion of parent partnerships to improve outcomes for transitioning youth?

The preceding chapters in this book summarize recent research findings and suggest actions practitioners can take to engage parents in the five roles. Parents who are collaborators with schools and agencies as they plan and implement collaborative strategies will provide a strengthened network of support for youth to achieve individual goals within those systems. Parents prepared to be instructors to their youth as they emerge as leaders in their own life will reinforce self-determination and self-advocacy skills across many environments both in and outside of school and service delivery. They will support these young adults to understand the ramifications of their disabilities and disclose and advocate for accommodations as appropriate in school, further education, and employment. Parents who serve with practitioners as evaluators and decision makers regarding their own child's program provide insightful questions and appraisal to the system based on their "whole person" perspective. In addition, they provide valuable viewpoints related to the system serving their child, both informally and through formal parent surveys and advisory boards. Parents who emerge as peer mentors for other parents will provide information and "I've been there" perspectives that will strengthen the engagement of parents who are newly facing the issues of transition. Finally, parents who courageously step forward taking actions that will change the system will earn the appreciation of those who will benefit from future improvements to the system.

Use of Evaluative Tools in This Book

Both the No Child Left Behind Act of 2001 (NCLB) and the Individuals With Disabilities Education Improvement Act of 2004 (IDEA) have a strong focus on accountability; we have created a set of tools that practitioners can use to engage parents as well as to measure their own effectiveness and the degree of improvement in facilitating parent empowerment. First, Pleet developed the Parent Transition Information Needs Survey (Appendix A), which can be sent to parents prior to individualized education program (IEP) meetings that will include discussion of transition. This survey will alert both parents and the practitioners about topics to be discussed in more detail or information to be provided to parents. Second, Pleet developed the Degree of Involvement Scale (Appendix B) that practitioners and parents can use collaboratively to identify individual parents' current levels of involvement in each of five roles. Practitioners can use this information to determine each parent's individual degree of involvement and use the findings as a basis of conversation about opportunities for parents to become more engaged. Third, schools or programs can use the Parent Engagement Strategic Planning Guide (Appendix C) to identify current and potential activities to build empowering partnerships with parents in the five focused roles. Further guidance on the use of these tools to enhance accountability activities is provided at the end of this chapter. We encourage practitioners to adapt these tools to their own situation and needs as they build stronger parent engagement practices that will contribute to the achievement of positive student outcomes.

Making Parent Partnerships a Priority

Review of Current Federal Legislation

Federal legislation currently requires that schools report accountability data. Schools are held accountable under both NCLB and IDEA. Both pieces of legislation have a multitude of requirements and expectations for states and school districts (National Education Association, 2004). NCLB has five areas of major concern to special educators (i.e., assessments, accountability, interventions, teacher quality, and paraeducator quality), has influenced responsive language within IDEA, and has established mechanisms to monitor and evaluate the evolution and the efficacy of those practices. For example, under NCLB's adequate yearly progress (AYP) provisions, state and district objectives must establish annual performance targets for all students, including students with disabilities. NCLB also requires documentation, as a part of its annual progress review, that each local education agency (LEA) receiving Title I, Part A funds, is, among other things, carrying out its responsibilities with respect to parental involvement.

The U.S. Department of Education (ED) publication *Parental Involvement* (2004) describes NCLB parent involvement provisions:

The No Child Left Behind Act of 2001 (NCLB Act) reauthorized the Elementary and Secondary Education Act of 1965 (ESEA), and is based on four principles that provide a framework through which families, educators, and communities can work together to improve teaching and learning. These principles are accountability for results, local control and flexibility, expanded parental choice, and effective and successful programs that reflect scientifically based research. The parental involvement provisions in Title I, Part A of the ESEA reflect these principles. Specifically, these provisions stress shared accountability between schools and parents for high student achievement, including expanded public school choice and supplemental educational services for eligible children in low-performing schools, local development of parental involvement plans with sufficient flexibility to address local needs, and building parents' capacity for using effective practices to improve their own children's academic achievement. (p. 1)

Under these provisions, each LEA must develop an improvement plan that includes their strategies for involving parents, including how they will (1) involve parents in jointly developing school improvement plan; (2) provide the coordination, technical assistance, and other support necessary to assist Title I, Part A schools in planning and implementing effective parental involvement activities to improve student academic achievement and school performance; (3) build the schools' and parents' capacity for strong parental involvement; (4) coordinate and integrate parental involvement strategies under Title I, Part A with parental involvement strategies under other programs, such as Head Start, Reading First, . . . (5) conduct, with the involvement of parents, an annual evaluation of the content and effectiveness of the parental involvement policy in improving the academic quality of the schools served with Title I, Part A funds, including—(a) Identifying barriers to greater participation by parents in parental involvement activities, with particular attention to parents who are economically disadvantaged, are disabled, have limited English proficiency, have limited literacy, or are of any racial or ethnic minority background; (b) Using the findings of the evaluation to design strategies for more effective parental involvement; (c) Revising, if necessary, the LEA's parental involvement policies; and (6) involve parents in the activities of schools served under Title I, Part A. [Section 1118(a)(2), ESEA]

In addition, state education agencies (SEAs) must publicize and disseminate the results of an annual review of progress for each school to its LEAs, teachers and other staff, parents, students, and the community and publicize parents' rights to informed school choice (ED, 2004).

There are no corresponding sections in IDEA regarding AYP for students with disabilities, but IDEA strongly intersects with the NCLB accountability focus relative to its own practices. Under IDEA, ED's Office of Special Education Programs (OSEP) monitors state departments of education using quantifiable indicators in each of three priority areas: (a) provision of a free appropriate public education in the least restrictive environment; (b) exercise of general supervisory authority, including child find, effective monitoring, the use of resolution sessions, mediation, voluntary binding arbitration, and a system of transition services; and (c) disproportionate representation of racial and ethnic groups in special education and related services, to the extent the representation is the result of inappropriate identification. The first priority area reflects graduation/dropout rates, assessment performance, suspension/expulsion, education placements, preschool outcomes, and parent participation. The second priority area addresses evaluation timelines, IDEA complaints, and due process (including mediation and resolution, general supervision systems, and transition at the preschool, secondary, and postsecondary levels). Finally, the third priority area focuses on disproportional identification of eligibility for special education services in general, as well as disaggregated by disability categories. To gather data related to these three priority areas, OSEP established a set of 20 Part B performance indicators by which states can quantifiably measure and report their progress towards meeting expected practices.

Each state is required to submit an annual performance report, which measures and reports on the state's progress in meeting the targets and goals specified in their state performance plan (SPP), to OSEP. According to OSEP Part B Indicators, States must submit (a) progress data and improvement activities and (b) an indication of the Web site where a complete copy of the state's revised SPP is available. State data collection tools and sampling plans must be approved by OSEP. Any formative changes made to the SPP regarding revised targets, activities, timelines, or resources linked to Indicator data collection or interpretation must include justification. Revisions to targets, activities, timelines or resources do not relieve the state of its responsibility to provide "actual target data" for the given year (ED, n.d.).

Of the 20 Part B performance indicators, there are 4 that speak specifically to secondary transition planning and postsecondary outcomes (see box, "Performance Indicators Relating to Secondary Transition Planning"). No other indicators refer specifically to the secondary transition aspect of special education, including the one pertinent to this book, Indicator 8, which addresses percentage of parents with a child receiving special education services who report that schools facilitated parent involvement as a means of improving services and results for children with disabilities.

Indicator 8 actually possesses a bifurcated assessment focus, in that its intent is to measure parent participation in IDEA Part C services (early intervention) as well as in Part B services (K–12). The language noted above is that for Part B services, which—although not specifically focusing on transition issues—has great relevance to the secondary transition planning years.

It is significant that both NCLB and IDEA support accountability with parent participation, as a validation of the extensive research into the benefits of parent partnerships. Prior chapters in this book delineate the significant contributions that parents can make to transition planning and implementation. However, each chapter goes beyond traditional measures of parent satisfaction with their participation and into the realm of empowered parents as collaborators, instructors, evaluators and decision makers, peer mentors, and systems change agents. Hence, if parent *partnerships*, as opposed to parent *participation,* are to be fully realized, we believe that Indicator 8 data should be used in tandem with other measures to examine the effectiveness of current practices and develop strategic plans for parent

PERFORMANCE INDICATORS RELATING TO SECONDARY TRANSITION PLANNING

Indicator 1: Percent of youth with IEPs graduating from high school with a regular diploma compared to percent of all youth in the state graduating with a regular diploma.

Indicator 2: Percent of youth with IEPs dropping out of high school compared to the percent of all youth in the state dropping out of high school.

Indicator 13: Percent of youth aged 16 and above with an IEP that includes coordinated, measurable, annual IEP goals and transition services that will reasonably enable the student to meet the post-secondary goals.

Indicator 14: Percent of youth who had IEPs, are no longer in secondary school and who have been competitively employed, enrolled in some type of post-secondary school, or both, within one year of leaving high school.

engagement. Local districts and schools could then clearly delineate discrete behaviors and actions that more closely embrace building reciprocal parent partnerships across K to 12 services and as a bridge to postschool outcomes for these parents' young adults. We believe that two benchmarks of an accountability system to guide incorporation of parent partnerships into school improvement should be (a) specificity in measuring parent participation in terms of proactive roles defined in this book, and (b) strong evidence that schools are taking actions to empower parents in those roles.

Examination of existing NCLB data on parent participation across the entire school population reveals that schools may not only be failing to empower parents, but also many were failing to include any related action in their improvement activities. For example, although NCLB spells out parent involvement requirements for schools in need of improvement, the majority (54%) of the reviewed Northwest Region school improvement plans failed to include specific activities. Many schools relied only on communication as the primary way to involve parents, despite the wide range of parent involvement practices discussed in the literature. (Regional Education Laboratory, 2008). In addition to NCLB data collection on parent participation, LEAs and SEAs are now beginning to report data related to IDEA Indicator 8. Local entities looked to a federally funded resource center for guidance in methodology and instruments to collect data related to parent satisfaction with their involvement.

Indicator 8 Assessment

To comply with Indicator 8 data collection, states must show they are using statistically robust tools to measure parent participation. The use of parent surveys has emerged as the preferred choice, and the National Center for Special Education Accountability Monitoring (NCSEAM) has responded with survey templates for states to access. Each state using the NCSEAM template has autonomy in determining which items to include in their survey, as well as what types of sampling techniques to use. In a review of the 2007 SPPs as approved by OSEP, 43 states and territories used all or part of the NCSEAM survey template.

The NCSEAM survey template contains a wide range of items with instructions indicating that the administration of 25 items per scale is adequate to ensure high reliability of measures. The NCSEAM survey templates contain several item subsets. The School Efforts to Partner with Parents Scale (SEPPS) directly addresses the Part B indicator; it comprises parent perceptions of (a) general services, (b) teacher and administrator outreach and partnerships, and (c) the school's outreach and partnerships. Additional items that replicate items with the Part C (Infants and Toddlers) survey are available and measure parental perceptions of (a) quality of services by teachers, administrators, and the school; (b) impact of special education services on the family; and (c) levels of parent participation in their children's learning, school organizations, and systemic change activities.

Examination of NSCEAM Items Relative to the Five Parent Engagement Roles

Because the SEPPS section of the NCSEAM survey tool speaks specifically to Part B services and therefore is more pertinent to the transition planning ages, we examined it relative to our five parent roles. Within those items, there is a trend to depict parents as being in reactive, receptive modes rather than proactive partnership roles. Specifically, the language in the primary, more general SEPPS section revolves around "I was offered," "I was given," "I received," and so forth. Items indicating a partnership (e.g., "I am considered an equal partner with teachers and other professionals in planning my child's program," "Teachers treat me as a team member") are seemingly ambiguous in delineating what an equal partnership or a team membership is, which leaves the perceptions of the parents in a precarious relationship to how the schools may interpret that same term. Other items ask about parents' presence in discussions (participating in assessments, accommodations, etc.), but do not indicate any balance of ownership or leadership of such discussions. Finally, school efforts in creating procedural documents reflect their ownership of the documents and their transmittal to parents ("My child's evaluation report was written in language I understand," "Written justification was given for the extent that my child would not receive services in the regular classroom"), rather than a collaborative or even parent-influenced context. Under the Teachers and Administrators section of the SEPPS, the statements show a more egalitarian approach, measuring professional sensitivity to cultural heritage and the needs of students with disabilities and their families. However, those measures are not action-oriented, as in the first section, and therefore indicate no opportunity for collaborative reciprocity. Statements within that section that are action-oriented, again, seem to cast the school as the authority and parents as the recipients rather than empowered leaders in the process ("Teachers and administrators ensure that I have fully understood the Procedural Safeguards," "Teachers and administrators encourage me to participate in the decision-making process"). Finally, in the last subset of the SEPPS, parents are asked to rate the school on their efforts, and replicate the "parent as recipient" voice ("communicates regularly with me regarding my student's progress on IEP goals," "offers parents training about special education issues," "offers parents a variety of ways to communicate with teachers," and "provides information on agencies that can assist my child").

Although these items collect data about whether parents receive information necessary to become partners in their child's special education services (and, correspondingly, in their transition-related aspects), we believe they do not investigate measures that will contribute to parent partnerships in their truest sense. Although the information schools and school professionals offer parents is essential, it does not in and of itself establish a collaborative, reciprocal, or balanced partnership that empowers parents to serve as collaborators, instructors, evaluators and decision makers, peer mentors, or systems change agents. Some may argue that a parent survey can be a viable vehicle for gathering parents' evaluative perspectives, yet it does not necessarily establish a venue for reciprocal responsive discussion of the effectiveness of current practices.

One section of the NCSEAM template, the Parent Participation subset, does reflect possible venues for identifying proactive parental roles as instructors through measures using statements such as "I engage in learning activities with my child at home" and "I ask my child to talk about what he or she is learning in school." Further, items are available that might depict a parent as an evaluator or a change agent ("I am part of a school advisory committee," "I am part of a district-level/state level special education committee," "I follow changes in the federal and state laws that affect special education," "I work with others to improve the special education system"); as a mentor ("I attend training sessions relating to the needs of children with disabilities," "I participate in an organization for parents of children with disabilities"); or as a collaborator ("I value the school's input concerning my child," "I meet with my child's teachers to plan my child's program and services"). Although these items do not provide more specific delineations of those actions, they are significant actions that validate the premise that parents can be proactive participants and partners in the special education process.

We emphatically applaud current goals and practices in identifying and quantifying the important contributions that parents make during the school years. Although the involvement of parents of children with disabilities was mandated with the inception of in the Education of All Handicapped Children Act of 1975, it is only recently that schools have been held accountable to systematically measure and report parent satisfaction levels, and the shift is gratifying. We submit for consideration in this process, particularly within the context of transition services, additional assessment and strategic planning tools that LEAs and SEAs can use to evaluate their own parent engagement practices in specific roles as described in the preceding chapters, as well as to conduct action planning to enhance parent and student empowerment in those roles. Although these instruments and resulting data are informal in nature and therefore may not become formal parts of SPPs, we believe they will assist practitioners in schools in assessing, critiquing, planning, and facilitating empowerment of parents in specific definable and measurable partnership roles during transition planning and implementation. Further, community and adult service practitioners may find these tools easily adaptable in support of their commitment to engage parents as partners in the transition process.

Tools for Strategically Building Parent Partnerships

The Parent Transition Information Needs Survey (Appendix A) can be sent to parents prior to transition-related meetings, with the intent that responses will inform practitioner sensitivity to information and interaction needs and preferences; this in turn will set the stage for empowering parents to contribute to the creation of a collaborative environment. This survey will alert both parents and the practitioners about topics to be discussed in more detail or informative materials to be provided to parents.

Practitioners and parents can collaboratively use the Degree of Involvement Scale (Appendix B) to identify individual parents' current involvement levels in each of the five roles. This information can provide the foundation for opportunities for parents to become more engaged. When a practitioner–parent team completes this assessment relative to that parent's engagement, the results can be used to plan ways to increase role empowerment for the individual parent. In this collaborative process, practitioners must remember that individual parents present unique needs, skills, awareness, and availability. It is neither expected nor desirable for all parents to operate at high levels of engagement in all roles; instead, each parent should be empowered to be engaged at levels that are specifically appropriate for their individual situations. A practitioner who is sensitive to parent differences will use professional judgment to empower parents to expand their engagement as desired.

If this assessment is completed with all parents with whom a practitioner professionally interacts, it allows an aggregated picture of current role-specific parent partnership levels and projects possible trends and patterns. The opportunity for this level of practitioner awareness surpasses simple satisfaction data and can be a bridge to systemic transformation.

Finally, schools can use the Parent Engagement Strategic Planning Guide (Appendix C) to identify their current engagement practices and design outreach efforts that foster balanced, equitable, and respectful partnerships with parents in the five focused roles. Aggregated data from the Degree of Involvement Scale can substantially inform strategic planning teams of current parent levels of involvement. These teams, incorporating parent voice, must have the commitment to facilitate parents' desired roles as they move towards joint ownership of the transition programming process.

We have focused these tools for educators and school systems to use as they enhance their partnerships with parents; however, we believe that agencies can adapt our tools and process for their own purposes. Although adult agencies specifically direct their services to the adult "client" and will only include parents and other supportive adults in their service provision if the client gives permission, it is widely accepted that these young adults continue to need and use support from their parents throughout much of their adulthood. We believe that adult agencies that strategically engage and empower parents in the five roles will increase the success of their adult clients.

Final Words

As we look at the ultimate purpose of building partnerships with parents, we must come back to student outcomes. IDEA states that the purpose of special education is "to ensure that all children with disabilities have available to them a free appropriate public education that emphasizes special education and related services designed to meet their unique needs and prepare them for further education, employment, and independent living" (20 U.S.C. §1400(c)(5)(A)(i)). Joined with the context of NCLB, students are to have access to and make progress in the general curriculum to the maximum extent appropriate. These requirements create a vision of youth with disabilities participating in appropriately rigorous instruction, and preparing for an "enviable" (Gaylord, Agosta, Barclay, Melda, & Stenhjem, 2006) adult life in which they are enabled to truly be full citizens of their inclusive communities. The future economy of our country cannot settle for less. If we are to impact disappointing statistics about employment of adults with disabilities, we must engage all stakeholders. Youth must be prepared to understand the implications of their disabilities, they must learn to disclose and advocate for needed accommodations appropriately, and most important, they must assume ownership for their own success. Schools cannot achieve this vision alone. Over two decades of research has substantiated the impact parents can have on student success (Epstein, 2005). But most parents will not take the initiative to step forward. As their children enter adolescence, they are new to the discussions of transition, and they are looking for guidance, information, and support; but they bring with them a wealth of personal experience as parents and as functioning adults in their employment and community activities. With encouragement, parents will step into opportunities to learn and contribute to their own child and the systems that engage them. It will take focused strategic planning and implementation, but the work will be worth it.

We have a mission. We advocate for a world in which parents and practitioners work together as partners to support and empower youth with disabilities to develop their potential to the fullest. In this essential existence, practitioners value and support diverse parents and families as partners in planning, instruction, evaluation, and systems change activities. Practitioners build on the possibility of working as team members rather than competitors. Parents are confident that practitioners are working with them and do not have to threaten legal action to be heard. Practitioners grow in their sensitivity to home-based issues impacting their students and clients on a daily basis. Practitioners continually assess their own actions and values in the process of critically improving their professionalism. Parents and practitioners are willing to be simultaneous leaders and followers in the collaborative process. Ultimately, parents and practitioners revel in shared communication, and celebrate the successes they have collaboratively fostered in the young adult's achievements. The intention of this book is to awaken your powers to achieve this mission.

REFERENCES

Epstein, J. L. (2005). *Developing and sustaining research-based programs of school, family, and community partnerships: Summary of five years of NNPS research.* Baltimore: National Network of Partnership Schools.

Gaylord, V., Agosta, J., Barclay, J., Melda, K., & Stenhjem, P. (Eds.). (2006, Spring/ Summer). *Impact: Feature Issue on Parenting Teens and Young Adults with Disabilities, 19*(2). Minneapolis: University of Minnesota, Institute on Community Integration.

Individuals With Disabilities Education Improvement Act of 2004, 20 U.S.C. §1400 *et seq.* (2004).

National Education Association. (2004). *The intersection of IDEA and NCLB.* Washington, DC: Author.

No Child Left Behind Act of 2001, 20 U.S.C. § 6301 *et seq.* (2002).

Regional Education Laboratory. (2008). *Parent involvement activities in school improvement plans in the northwest region.* Washington, DC: Institute of Educational Sciences.

United States Department of Education. (2004). *Parental Involvement: Title I, Part A Non-Regulatory Guidance.* Washington, DC: Author. Available from www.ed.gov/ programs/titleiparta/parentinvguid.doc

U.S. Department of Education. (n.d.). *Part C State Performance Plan (SPP) for 2004-2011 Instruction Sheet* (OMB No. 1820-0624). Retrieved November 18, 2008, from http://www.ed.gov/policy/speced/guid/idea/capr/2008/1cinstsheet081908.pdf

ABOUT THE AUTHORS

DONNA L. WANDRY is an Associate Professor of Special Education at West Chester University of Pennsylvania. Dr. Wandry has served children and youth with disabilities directly in school and agency settings. She was the Project Director for a federal systems change transition grant while serving as the Transition Coordinator at the Kansas Board of Education, and has taught transition coursework at both the undergraduate and graduate levels in higher education for 15 years. She is a national Past President of the Council for Exceptional Children's Division on Career Development and Transition. Her primary areas of interest are special education legislation and movement from school to adult life for persons with disabilities, with a focus on working with families and providers to create systemic changes that facilitate that movement.

AMY M. PLEET has over 35 years of experience as an English Teacher, Special Education Teacher, Transition Specialist (district and state department), higher education faculty (Special Education Graduate Director and Associate Professor) and now Secondary Inclusion Consultant with the University of Delaware to districts committed to improving the effectiveness of instruction for included students with disabilities. As the parent of two young adults with disabilities, Dr. Pleet is especially aware of a parent's perspectives and the contributions they can make. Her research and writing focus on building parent partnerships, self-determination, and inclusionary secondary school reform.

APPENDIX A

Parent Transition Information Needs Survey

This survey is designed to be completed by parents in preparation for transition discussions at IEP and agency meetings. Practitioners may want to review the completed survey prior to the meeting so that they can prepare for discussion of needed information

I would like to learn more about . . .	This is a priority!	I would like more information now	Maybe later	No information needed
1. my rights (the procedural safeguards) in the IEP process.				
2. my adolescent's disability, specifically how it affects his/her learning and what accommodations and/or technology might be appropriate in different placement options.				
3. how I can support my adolescent as he/she develops IEP or ITP goals and takes ownership of his/her educational and future success.				
4. high school graduation requirements and the choices my adolescent will have within this high school program.				
5. Age of Majority guidelines that will give my adolescent legal rights in this state and what they will mean for us.				
6. vocational rehabilitation and other adult service systems that my adolescent may be eligible for after high school.				
7. laws that protect civil rights for adults with disabilities (i.e., Americans with Disability Act and Rehabilitation Act).				
8. disability support services that are available in postsecondary institutions and how they are different from high school.				
9. parent support groups and mentors (also parents of youth with disabilities) who will listen to my concerns and provide me information and support.				
10. opportunities for me to provide feedback to the school and system about what they are doing right as well as areas for improvement.				
11. opportunities for me to become a mentor to other parents just beginning the transition process.				
12. opportunities for me to become a leader in school improvement or systems change, using what I have learned as a parent.				

From *Engaging and Empowering Families in Secondary Transition: A Practitioner's Guide.* Copyright 2009 CEC. This page may be photocopied for individual, classroom, or small group work only.

From *Engaging and Empowering Families in Secondary Transition: A Practitioner's Guide.* Copyright 2009 CEC. This page may be photocopied for individual, classroom, or small group work only.

APPENDIX B

Degree of Involvement Scale

Part I: Consider what you know about what this parent brings

– information about the child's disability?

– family socio-economic, cultural situation?

– family's level of coping with disability?

– family's engagement with resources outside of school/program?

Part II: Analyze degree of involvement in each role

– Parents as collaborators in the IEP process

1	2	3	4	5
Don't attend Unaware of IEP	Passive at team	Attend team Agree with plan	Attend team Question plan	Contribute to plan

– Parents as instructors in their youths' emergent independence

1	2	3	4	5
Not aware of goals on IEP	Teach youth basic household chores	Foster skills for independence	Help reinforce IEP goals at home	Foster self determination & personal leadership

– Parents as decision maker/evaluators

1	2	3	4	5
Unaware of plan	Passive acceptance at team	Provide evaluation of youth's IEP	Respond to requests for program evaluation	Serves on program/system evaluation group

– Parents as peer mentors

1	2	3	4	5
No involvement with other parents	Listen to other parents	Seek other parents Join support group	A leader in parent support group	Speaker/trainer for parents

– Parents as system change agents

1	2	3	4	5
Unaware of system issues	Awareness/ opinion of system issues	Sign petitions Write letters	Advocate for change in local school	Advocate for change in system/state/ region

APPENDIX C

Parent Engagement Strategic Planning Guide

This is a tool for collaborative program self-evaluation and strategic planning. As you consider the evidence based strategies in each chapter of this monograph, use this tool as a guide for planning how to expand your program's engagement of parents.

Rating scale: 1 = no practices   2 = one activity   3 = occasional strategies
4 = 1–2 regular strategies   5 = regular multiple strategies

Parents as	What we are doing now	Possible actions	First step	Lead stakeholder
Collaborators in the IEP Process 1 2 3 4 5				
Instructors in Their Youth's Emergent Independence 1 2 3 4 5				
Decision Makers & Evaluators 1 2 3 4 5				
Peer Mentors 1 2 3 4 5				
Systems Change Agents 1 2 3 4 5				

From *Engaging and Empowering Families in Secondary Transition: A Practitioner's Guide.* Copyright 2009 CEC. This page may be photocopied for individual, classroom, or small group work only.